The BOOK
of CLASSIC
INSULTS

The BOOK
of CLASSIC
INSULTS

Edited by Tom Steele

Quill
William Morrow
New York

Library of Congress Cataloging-in-Publication Data

The book of classic insults / edited by Tom Steele.
p.   cm.
"A Quill original."
ISBN 0-688-15907-9 (alk. paper)
1. Invective Humor.   I. Steele, Tom, 1952–
PN6231.I65B59   1999
808.88'2—dc21   99-15167
CIP

Printed in the United States of America

First Edition

3   4   5   6   7   8   9   10

BOOK DESIGN BY JO ANNE METSCH

www.williammorrow.com

CONTENTS

Contents

INTRODUCTION

ALL HUMOR IS funny at the expense of someone
or something. Insults are the pungent distillation of this
concept. Therefore, probably nothing is funnier than a
well-conceived insult.

And perhaps we love tried-and-true insults so much because they provide such intense relief from that gnawing
sensation that torments us when we've been reduced to
thinking, "What I *should* have said. . . ."

Here are hundreds and hundreds of the sharpest invectives
we could find in the history of verbal abuse. Many of the
insult hurlers are world famous; some are far less famous
than the insult they delivered. Some of the insults were in
writing, some were delivered live and impromptu; some are
centuries old, most are more recent, and some were pro-
nounced last week. But they all have one thing in common:
They are the funniest and most inspiring excoriations in the
English language.

The BOOK
of CLASSIC
INSULTS

APPEARANCE

. . . .

"She got her looks from her father. He's a plastic surgeon."

Groucho Marx

"All God's children are not beautiful. Most of God's children are, in fact, barely presentable."

Fran Lebowitz

"She was what we used to call a suicide blonde—dyed by her own hand."

Saul Bellow

"My mother-in-law had plastic surgery. She had a little work done on her nose . . . they put it in the middle of her face."

Redd Foxx

"He left his body to science—and science is contesting the will."

David Frost

"[Alexander Woollcott] looked like something that had gotten loose from Macy's Thanksgiving Day Parade."

Harpo Marx

"[William Paley] looks like a man who has just swallowed an entire human being."

Truman Capote

"You know, you have very beautiful children. It's a good thing your wife cheats on you."

Joey Bishop

"I was one of the few brides who ever got a request from the congregation to keep the veil on."

Phyllis Diller

"As you get older, the pickings get slimmer, but the people don't."

Carrie Fisher

"Whenever I see his fingernails, I thank God I don't have to look at his feet."

British actress Athene Seyler
on journalist Hannen Swaffer

While taking the Grand Tour, "when you look like your passport photo, it's time to go home."
Erma Bombeck

"Prince Charles's ears are so big he could hang-glide over the Falklands."
Joan Rivers

Actor Roger Moore described Joan Rivers as "a depressed area's Don Rickles—only not as pretty."

"[Don Rickles] looks like an extra in a crowd scene by Hieronymus Bosch."
Kenneth Tynan

"He's so fat his bathtub has stretch marks."
*Orlando Magic manager Pat Williams,
describing basketball player Charles Barkley*

"[Princess Anne is] such an active lass. So outdoorsy. She loves nature in spite of what it did to her."
Bette Midler

"She looked as if she had been poured into her clothes and had forgotten to say 'when.'"
P. G. Wodehouse

A certain actress told Rosalind Russell, "I dread the thought of forty-five." Russell replied, "Why? What happened to you then, dear?"

"Her hat is a creation that will never go out of style. It will look ridiculous year after year."
Fred Allen

"She has a face like a well-kept grave."
Tory MP on
Labour MP Shirley Summerskill

"I have a face that is a cross between two pounds of halibut and an explosion in an old clothes cupboard."
David Niven

George Bernard Shaw on Isadora Duncan:
"A woman whose face looked as if it had been made of sugar and someone had licked it."

"To me, Edith [Evans] looks like something that would eat its young."
Dorothy Parker

"I'm not saying this in a negative way, but honestly, do you really think that Hillary or Bill Clinton, from what you can see, is very concerned about their appearance?"
Christophe, Hairdresser-to-the-Stars

"The only reason my mother-in-law wasn't on Noah's ark was because they couldn't find another animal that looked like her."

Phyllis Diller

"My mother-in-law has such a big mouth that when she smiles, there's lipstick on her ears."

Redd Foxx

"The man was so small, he was a waste of skin."

Fred Allen

"I'm tired of all this nonsense about beauty being only skin deep. That's deep enough. What do you want, an adorable pancreas?"

Jean Kerr

"I have a face that looks like an elephant's behind. It would stop a sundial."

Charles Laughton

"You know you've reached middle age when someone tells you to pull in your stomach and you just did."

Milton Berle

"Your mother is so fat, she thinks gravy is a beverage."

James Percelay, Monteria Ivey, and Stephan Dweck, Triple Snaps

"Governor [Lester] Maddox has the face of a three-month-old infant who is mean and bald and wears eyeglasses."
Norman Mailer

George Bush's campaign press secretary, Torie Clarke, on Ross Perot:
"Heckuva guy. I have a hard time relating to somebody whose wingspan with his ears is wider than his total height."

"The Russians love Brooke Shields because her eyebrows remind them of Leonid Brezhnev."
Robin Williams

"On my honeymoon, Fang told me to unbutton my pajamas, and I wasn't wearing any."
Phyllis Diller

"You're so ugly, when you were a child even your imaginary friends wouldn't play with you."
James Percelay, Monteria Ivey, and Stephan Dweck, Triple Snaps

Howard Hughes on Clark Gable:
"His ears make him look like a taxicab with both doors open."

"Your mother is so ugly, she could make an onion cry."
George Wallace, on
The Arsenio Hall Show

Joan Rivers on Elizabeth Taylor:
"Is she fat? Her favorite food is seconds. . . . She puts mayonnaise on an aspirin."

Elizabeth Taylor to Kim Novak, in *The Mirror Crack'd:*
"You know, there are two things I can't stand about you. Your face."

"Elizabeth Taylor looks like two small boys fighting underneath a thick blanket."
Earl Blackwell

"Your brother is so short, he couldn't hi-five a Smurf."
James Percelay, Monteria Ivey,
and Stephan Dweck, Triple Snaps

"Oh, my God, look at you! Anyone else hurt in the accident?"
Don Rickles,
to Ernest Borgnine

"Phyllis Diller had so many face-lifts there's nothing left in her shoes."
Bob Hope

"Never trust a man who combs his hair straight from his left armpit."
Alice Roosevelt Longworth

Journalist David Frye on President Gerald Ford:
"He looks like the guy in a science fiction movie who is the
first to see the Creature."

"Your sister is so ugly, she has to sneak up on her mirror."
James Percelay, Monteria Ivey,
and Stephan Dweck, Triple Snaps

"Glenda Jackson has a face to launch a thousand dredgers."
Jack de Manio

"He doesn't dye his hair, he's just prematurely orange."
Gerald Ford, on Ronald Reagan

"[Robert Redford] has turned almost alarmingly blond—
he's gone past platinum, he must be in plutonium; his hair
is coordinated with his teeth."
Pauline Kael

"[Mick Jagger] has child-bearing lips."
Joan Rivers

THE BATTLE OF THE SEXES

. . . .

"Marriage [is] the most advanced form of warfare in the modern world."

Malcolm Bradbury

"The music at a wedding procession always reminds me of the music of soldiers going into battle."

Heinrich Heine

"My wife and I were happy for twenty years. Then we met."

Rodney Dangerfield

"I love being married. It's so great to find that one special person you want to annoy for the rest of your life."

Rita Rudner

"If you can stay in love for more than two years, you're *on* something."

Fran Lebowitz

"I couldn't see tying myself down to a middle-aged woman with four children, even though the woman was my wife and the children were my own."

Joseph Heller

"Never feel remorse for what you have thought about your wife. She has thought much worse things about you."

Jean Rostand

"The last woman I had sex with just hated me. I could tell by the way she asked for the money."

Drew Carey

"The prostitute is the only honest woman left in America."

Ti-Grace Atkinson

Roseanne on why she and her ex-husband Tom Arnold didn't have a child:
"We were trying to get pregnant, but I forgot one of us had to have a penis."

"Why are married women heavier than single women? Single women come home, see what's in the fridge, and go to bed. Married women come home, see what's in bed, and go to the fridge."

Anonymous

"The way to fight a woman is with your hat. Grab it and run."

John Barrymore

"I married beneath me; all women do."

Nancy Astor

"If variety is the spice of life, marriage is the big can of leftover Spam."

Johnny Carson

"The main difference between men and women is that men are lunatics and women are idiots."

Rebecca West

"It's better to have loved and lost than to have loved and married."

Sammy Shore

"Even hooligans marry, though they know that marriage is but for a little while. It is alimony that is forever."

Quentin Crisp

"Woman was God's second mistake."

Friedrich Nietzsche

"Sex is the biggest nothing of all time."

Andy Warhol

"Certain women should be struck together regularly like gongs."

Noël Coward,
in Private Lives

"Women want to know: Why is it difficult to find men who are sensitive, caring, and good-looking? Because they already have boyfriends."

Anonymous

"When a man steals your wife, there is no better revenge than to let him keep her."

Sacha Guitry

"What do men and sperm cells have in common? They both have a one-in-a-million chance of becoming a human being."

Anonymous

"We sleep in separate rooms, we have dinner apart, we take separate vacations. We're doing everything we can to keep our marriage together."

Henny Youngman

"Most of us grow up to be the kind of men our mothers warned us against."

Brendan Behan

"Some stuff does bother me about being married . . . like having a husband."

Roseanne

"We were happily married for eight months. Unfortunately, we were married for four and a half years."

Golfer Nick Faldo

"The big mistake that men make is that when they turn thirteen or fourteen and all of a sudden they've reached puberty, they believe that they like women. Actually, you're just horny. It doesn't mean you like women any more at twenty-one than you did at ten."

Jules Feiffer

"If you want to read a book about love and marriage, you've got to buy two separate books."

Alan King

"Why did nature create Man? Was it to show that she is big enough to make mistakes, or was it pure ignorance?"

Holbrook Jackson

"If you pick up a starving dog and make him prosperous, he will not bite you. That is the principal difference between a dog and a man."

Mark Twain

"If people waited to know each other before they were married, the world wouldn't be so grossly overpopulated."

W. Somerset Maugham

"Marriage: a ceremony in which rings are put on the finger of the lady and through the nose of the gentleman."

Herbert Spencer

"A woman drove me to drink, and I never even had the courtesy to thank her."

W. C. Fields

"The conventional [sexual] position makes me claustrophobic. And the others either give me a stiff neck or lockjaw."

Tallulah Bankhead

"Since I've been married, I don't have to worry about bad breath. I never get a chance to open my mouth."
Rodney Dangerfield

"A man is incomplete until he has married. Then he's finished."
Zsa Zsa Gabor

At a dinner party, Nancy Astor, peeved at Winston Churchill, told him, "Winston, if I were married to you, I'd put poison in your coffee." Churchill instantly replied, "Nancy, if you were my wife, I'd drink it."

"My wife's an earth sign. I'm a water sign. Together we make mud."
Rodney Dangerfield

"Few things can be less tempting or dangerous than a Greek woman of the age of thirty."
John Carne

"She's all right to look at, but intellectually I don't reckon she can tell her fishcakes from her falsies."
Alan Ayckbourn, in Sisterly Feelings

Mickey Rooney, who married eight times, once remarked, "Always get married early in the morning. That way, if it doesn't work out, you haven't wasted the whole day."

"Women would be more charming if one could fall into her arms without falling into her hands."

Ambrose Bierce

"Your wife is like TV. It's home and it's free."

Slappy White

"Husbands are like fires. They go out if unattended."

Zsa Zsa Gabor

"You don't know a woman until you've met her in court."

Norman Mailer

"His mother should have thrown him away and kept the stork."

Mae West

"Love is like cheap wine: It leads you to the stars, but leaves you with the gutrot of tomorrow."

British cartoonists
Chris Garratt and Mick Kidd

"Last week I told my wife, 'A man is like wine, he gets better with age.' She locked me in the cellar."

Rodney Dangerfield

"Love is the desire to prostitute oneself. There is, indeed, no exalted pleasure that cannot be related to prostitution."

Charles Baudelaire

"Marriage is a great institution, but I'm not ready for an institution."

Mae West

"The surest way to be alone is to get married."

Gloria Steinem

"I drink to your charm, your beauty, and your brains— which gives you a rough idea of how hard up I am for a drink."

Groucho Marx

"I know many married men, I even know a few happily married men, but I don't know one who wouldn't fall down the first open coal hole running after the first pretty girl who gave him a wink."

George Jean Nathan

"Marriage is like paying an endless visit in your worst clothes."

J. B. Priestley

"The more I see of men, the more I like dogs."

Madame de Staël

"There is a lot to say in her favor, but the other is more interesting."

Mark Twain

"When my wife was about to give birth, I said, 'Honey, if it looks like you, it would be great.' She said, 'If it looks like you, it'd be a miracle.' "

Rodney Dangerfield

"Love is the delightful interval between meeting a beautiful girl and discovering that she looks like a haddock."

John Barrymore

"The fastest way to a man's heart is through his chest."

Roseanne

Arnold Schwarzenegger said to Tom Arnold, "Listen, buddy, I only *play* the Terminator—you married one."

"Whatever women do they must do twice as well as men to be thought half as good. Luckily this is not difficult."

Charlotte Whitton

"I like men to behave like men: strong and childish."

Françoise Sagan

"A husband is what's left of the lover once the nerve has been extracted."

Helen Rowland

"Marriage is a romance in which the hero dies in the first chapter."

Anonymous

"The charms of a passing woman are usually in direct relation to the speed of her passing."

Marcel Proust

"Love is the delusion that one woman differs from another."
H. L. Mencken

"My husband's mind is like a Welsh railway: one track and dirty."

Anonymous

"Marriage is give and take. You'd better give it to her, or she'll take it anyway."

Joey Adams

"Women should be obscene and not heard."
Groucho Marx

"Girls bore me—they still do. I love Mickey Mouse more than any woman I've ever known."

Walt Disney

"Men are creatures with two legs and eight hands."

Jayne Mansfield

"Give a man a free hand and he'll run it all over you."

Mae West

"I hate women because they always know where things are."

James Thurber

"The only really happy folk are married women and single men."

H. L. Mencken

CHILDREN

. . . .

"Having a family is like having a bowling alley installed in your brain."

Martin Mull

"If pregnancy were a book, they would cut the last two chapters."

Nora Ephron

"The first half of our life is ruined by our parents, and the second half by our children."

Clarence Darrow

"Humans are the only animals that have children on purpose with the exception of guppies, who like to eat theirs."

P. J. O'Rourke

"I love children, especially when they cry, for then someone takes them away."

Nancy Mitford

"There's nothing relaxed about [children]. They're like these little tense things who scream in order to fall asleep. Just like adults, only more direct."

Ian Shoales

"If a child shows himself to be incorrigible, he should be decently and quietly beheaded at the age of twelve, lest he grow to maturity, marry, and perpetuate his kind."

Don Marquis

"Children are never too tender to be whipped. Like tough beefsteaks, the more you beat them, the more tender they become."

Edgar Allan Poe

"Children have been known to take a few years off your life—like fifty or sixty."

George Burns

"Children make the most desirable opponents in Scrabble, as they are both easy to beat and fun to cheat."

Fran Lebowitz

"Never raise your hand to your children; it leaves your mid-section unprotected."

Robert Orben

"Insanity is hereditary; you can get it from your children."

Sam Levenson

"Sometimes when I look at my children, I say to myself, 'Lillian, you should have stayed a virgin.' "

Lillian Carter

"Kids! I can't make them disappear, but I do wear dark glasses in the house hoping they won't recognize me."

Phyllis Diller

"My husband and I are either going to buy a dog or have a child. We can't decide whether to ruin our carpet or ruin our lives."

Rita Rudner

"Like its politicians and its wars, society has the teenagers it deserves."

J. B. Priestley

"I'm beginning to understand those animals you read about where the mother has got to hide the young so the father won't eat them."

W. C. Fields

"By the time the youngest children have learned to keep the house tidy, the oldest grandchildren are on hand to tear it to pieces."

Christopher Morley

"I could now afford all the things I never had as a kid, if I didn't have kids."

Robert Orben

"A grandfather is a man who can't understand how his idiot son had such brilliant children."

Milton Berle

"I was born by Cesarean section. This was the last time I had my mother's complete attention."

Richard Jeni

"When I get one of those 'mom' headaches, I take the advice on the aspirin bottle. Take two and keep away from children."

Roseanne

"I don't like the size of [children]; the scale is all wrong. The heads tend to be too big for the bodies and the hands and feet are a disaster and they keep falling into things. . . . They should be neither seen nor heard. And no one must make another one."

Gore Vidal

FRIE N DSHIP

. . . .

"May God defend me from my friends; I can defend myself from my enemies. . . . The one thing your friends will never forgive you is your happiness."

Albert Camus

"When a man takes to his bed, nearly all his friends have a secret desire to see him die; some to prove that his health is inferior to their own, others in the disinterested hope of being able to study a death agony."

Charles Baudelaire

"Every time a friend succeeds, I die a little."

Gore Vidal

"I never read bad reviews about myself because my best friends invariably tell me about them."

Oscar Levant

"We cherish our friends not for their ability to amuse us, but for ours to amuse them."

Evelyn Waugh

"People who get married because they're in love make a ridiculous mistake. It makes much more sense to marry your best friend. You *like* your best friend more than anyone you're ever going to be in love with."

Fran Lebowitz

"He's a self-made man . . . the living proof of the horrors of unskilled labor."

Ed Wynn

DOCTORS

. . . .

"Doctors are just the same as lawyers; the only difference is that lawyers merely rob you, whereas doctors rob you and kill you, too."

Anton Chekhov

"I almost think it is the ultimate destiny of science to exterminate the human race."

Thomas Love Peacock

"We may lay down a maxim, that when a nation abounds in physicians, it grows thin of people."

Joseph Addison

"The art of medicine consists in amusing the patient while nature cures the disease."

Voltaire

"A plastic surgeon is one who has credit card facilities."

Mike Barfield

"Freud is the father of psychoanalysis. It has no mother."

Germaine Greer

"Half of the modern drugs could well be thrown out of the window, except that the birds might eat them."

Dr. Martin Henry Fischer

"A male gynecologist is like an auto mechanic who has never owned a car."

Carrie Snow

LAWYERS

. . . .

"I do not come to speak ill of any man behind his back, but I believe the gentleman is an attorney."

Samuel Johnson

"A jury consists of twelve persons chosen to decide who has the better lawyer."

Robert Frost

"For certain people, after fifty, litigation takes the place of sex."

Gore Vidal

"I learned law so well, the day I graduated I sued the college, won the case, and got my tuition back."

Fred Allen

"An incompetent attorney can delay a trial for months or years. A competent attorney can delay one even longer."

Evelle J. Younger

"[Lawyers] are really an unnecessary profession. . . . What do they *do*? They don't produce anything. All they do is guide you through the labyrinth of the legal system that they created—and they keep changing it just in case you start to catch on."

Ian Shoales

"If law school is so hard to get through, how come there are so many lawyers?"

Calvin Trillin

"No brilliance is needed in the law. Nothing but common sense and relatively clean fingernails."

John Mortimer

"What's black and white and brown and looks good on a lawyer? A Doberman."

Mordecai Richler

WRITERS AND BOOKS

"Writers are a little below clowns and a little above trained seals."

John Steinbeck

"I have tried lately to read Shakespeare, and found it so intolerably dull that it nauseated me."

Charles Darwin

From Shaw:
"With the single exception of Homer, there is no eminent writer, not even Sir Walter Scott, whom I can despise so entirely as I despise Shakespeare when I measure my mind against his. The intensity of my impatience with him occasionally reaches such a pitch that it would positively be a relief to me to dig him up and throw stones at him, knowing as I do how incapable he and his worshippers are of understanding any less obvious form of indignity."

"[Jonathan Swift was] a monster gibbering shrieks, and gnashing imprecations against mankind, tearing down all shreds of modesty, past all sense of manliness and shame; filthy in word, filthy in thought, furious, raging, obscene."

William Thackeray

"Thackeray settled like a meat-fly on whatever one had got for dinner; and made one sick of it."

British writer John Ruskin

"[Henry Wadsworth] Longfellow is to poetry what the barrel organ is to music."

American critic Van Wyck Brooks

"[Percy Bysshe] Shelley should not be read, but inhaled through a gas pipe."

Lionel Trilling

George Eliot on Charlotte Brontë:
"I wish her characters would talk a little less like the heroes and heroines of police reports."

"[British poet Thomas Gray] was dull in company, dull in his closet, dull everywhere. He was dull in a new way, and that made many people think him GREAT. He was a mechanical poet."

Samuel Johnson

"Is Wordsworth a bell with a wooden tongue?"
Ralph Waldo Emerson

"Edgar Allan Poe's prose is unreadable—like Jane Austen's. No, there is a difference. I could read his prose on a salary, but not Jane's."
Mark Twain

"[Harriet Beecher Stowe's] *Uncle Tom's Cabin* was the first evidence to America that no hurricane can be so disastrous to a country as a ruthlessly humanitarian woman."
Sinclair Lewis

"Oscar Wilde's talent seems to me essentially rootless, something growing in a little glass of water."
British writer George Moore

"This awful Whitman. This post-mortem poet. This poet with the private soul leaking out of him all the time. All his privacy leaking out in a sort of dribble, oozing into the universe."
D. H. Lawrence

James Joyce's *Ulysses* is "a dogged attempt to cover the universe with mud, an inverted Victorianism, an attempt to make crossness and dirt succeed where sweetness and light failed, a simplification of the human character in the interests of hell."
E. M. Forster

Virginia Woolf found *Ulysses* "the work of a queasy under-graduate scratching his pimples."

American photographer Clover Adams on Henry James: "It's not that he bites off more than he can chew, but he chews more than he can bite off."

"Henry James has a mind so fine that no idea could violate it."

T. S. Eliot

"[Henry James was] one of the nicest old ladies I ever met."

William Faulkner

In a rejection letter for Marcel Proust's *Remembrance of Things Past,* Marc Humbolt wrote: "I may be dead from the neck up, but rack my brains as I may I can't see why a chap should need thirty pages to de-scribe how he turns over in bed before going to sleep."

"Reading Proust is like bathing in someone else's dirty water."

Alexander Woollcott

British actress Mrs. Patrick Campbell once said to George Bernard Shaw, "When you were a little boy, somebody ought to have said 'Hush' just once."

"[Shaw's] brain is a half-inch layer of champagne poured over a bucket of Methodist near-beer."

French writer Benjamin de Casseres

"Shaw is the most fraudulent, inept writer of Victorian melodrama ever to gull a timid critic or fool a dull public."

John Osborne

"In full regalia [Dame Edith Sitwell], looked like Lyndon B. Johnson dressed up like Elizabeth I."

Time *magazine, 1965*

"So you've been reviewing Edith Sitwell's latest piece of virgin dung, have you? Isn't she a poisonous thing of a woman, lying, concealing, flipping, plagiarizing, misquoting, and being as clever a crooked literary publicist as ever."

Dylan Thomas, writing to Glyn Jones in 1934

"[Dylan Thomas was] "an outstandingly unpleasant man, one who cheated and stole from his friends and peed on their carpets."

British novelist Kingsley Amis

"Free verse is like free love; it is a contradiction in terms."

G. K. Chesterton

"[W. Somerset Maugham] is a half-trashy novelist, who writes badly, but is patronized by half-serious readers, who do not care much about writing."

Edmund Wilson

"[George Orwell] would not blow his nose without moralizing on conditions in the handkerchief industry."

Cyril Connolly

"In the case of many poets, the most important thing for them to do is to write as little as possible."

T. S. Eliot

"I don't regard [Bertolt] Brecht as a man of iron-gray purpose and intellect, I think he is a theatrical whore of the first quality."

Peter Hall

"*Perfectly Scandalous* was one of those plays in which all of the actors unfortunately enunciated very clearly."

Robert Benchley

Sean O'Casey on P. G. Wodehouse:
"English literature's performing flea."

Dorothy Parker, in her "Constant Reader" column in *The New Yorker,* took on A. A. Milne: "And it is that word 'hummy,' my darlings, that marks the first place in *The House at Pooh Corner* at which Tonstant Weader Fwowed Up."

Dorothy Parker on a particularly odious best-seller:
"This is not a novel to be tossed aside lightly. It should be thrown with great force."

"I understand your play is full of single entendre."
George S. Kaufman,
to a fellow playwright

A press agent asked *Times* drama editor George S. Kaufman how he could get one of his clients' names into *The New York Times.* "Shoot her," Kaufman replied.

"It was a bad play saved by a bad performance."
George S. Kaufman

Alexander Woollcott on Dorothy Parker:
"A combination of Little Nell and Lady Macbeth."

When she was told that Clare Boothe Luce, the tart author of *The Women,* was always kind to her inferiors, Dorothy Parker asked, "Where does she find them?"

"Mr. [D. H.] Lawrence looked like a plaster gnome on a stone toadstool in some suburban garden. He looked as if he had just returned from spending an uncomfortable night in a very dark cave."

Dame Edith Sitwell

"Hemingway was a jerk."

Harold Robbins

"[Hemingway had] a literary style of wearing false hair on the chest."

Max Eastman

Gertrude Stein on Hemingway:
"Remarks are not literature."

"[Gertrude Stein] was a past master in making nothing happen very slowly."

Clifton Fadiman

"[E. M. Forster] is limp and damp and milder than the breath of a cow."

Virginia Woolf

"[W. H. Auden was] an engaging, bookish, American talent, too verbose to be memorable and too intellectual to be moving."

Philip Larkin

"One can't read any of Noël Coward's plays now; they are written in the most topical and perishable way imaginable; the cream in them turns sour overnight."

Cyril Connolly

"Under close scrutiny, [Carl] Sandburg's verse reminds us of the blobs of living jelly or plankton brought up by deep-sea dredging; it is a kind of protoplasmic poetry, lacking higher organization."

American critic George F. Whicher

Edmund Wilson on Carl Sandburg's *Lincoln*:
"The cruelest thing that has happened to Lincoln since he was shot by Booth has been to fall into the hands of Carl Sandburg."

Joseph Kraft on William Faulkner's writing:
"For my own part, I can rarely tell whether his characters are making love or playing tennis."

Clifton Fadiman on Clare Boothe Luce:
"No woman of our time has gone further with less mental equipment."

Here's how George S. Kaufman opened his review of an apparently disastrous comedy:
"There was laughter in the back of the theater, leading to the belief that someone was telling jokes back there."

"[Alexander Woollcott] was an emotionalist who rarely succumbed to the chill demands of logic. Woollcott was less a critic than an amusing hysteric."

Tallulah Bankhead

Groucho Marx told S. J. Perelman, about his first book, *Dawn Ginsberg's Revenge:*
"From the moment I picked up your book until I laid it down I was convulsed with laughter. Someday I intend reading it."

Gore Vidal on Herman Wouk's *Winds of War:*
"This is not at all bad, except as prose."

Truman Capote on Jack Kerouac:
"That's not writing, that's typing."

"Truman Capote has made lying an art. A minor art."

Gore Vidal

"I always said Little Truman had a voice so high it could only be detected by a bat."

Tennessee Williams

John Leonard on Gore Vidal's *Two Sisters:*
"He seems to have gone to his icebox, pulled out all the cold obsessions, mixed them in a bowl, beat too lightly and baked too long. . . . Aspiring to a soufflé, he achieves a pancake at which the reader saws without much attention. . . . There are too many ironies in the fire."

Norman Mailer to Gore Vidal:
"I've had to smell your works from time to time, and that has helped me to become an expert on intellectual pollution."

Richard Findlater on Lillian Hellman's *Toys in the Attic:*
"It is curious how incest, impotence, nymphomania, religious mania, and real estate speculation can be so dull."

"[J. D. Salinger is] the greatest mind ever to stay in prep school."

Norman Mailer

John Hollander on Allen Ginsberg's *Howl:*
"It is only fair to Allen Ginsberg to remark on the utter lack of decorum of any kind in this dreadful little volume. 'Howl' is meant to be a noun, but I can't help taking it as an imperative."

"The works of William Burroughs add up to the world's pluperfect put-on."

Time magazine

Poet/novelist James Dickey once said of Robert Frost, "If it were thought that anything I wrote was influenced by Robert Frost, I would take that particular piece of mine, shred it, and flush it down the toilet, hoping not to clog the pipes."

In 1955, the *Chicago Sun Times* reviewed William Gaddis's *The Recognitions* thusly:
"An evil book, a scurrilous book, a profane book, a scatological book, and an exasperating book. What this squalling overwritten book needs above all is to have its mouth washed out with lye soap. It reeks of decay and filth and perversion and half-digested learning."

On Joseph Heller's *God Knows:*
"It even looks like a real book, with pages and print and dust jacket and everything. This disguise is extremely clever, considering the contents; the longest lounge act never performed in the history of the Catskills."

Paul Gray

Gloria Steinem on Jacqueline Susann's *Valley of the Dolls:*
"For the reader who has put away comic books but isn't ready for editorials in the *Daily News*."

Jacqueline Susann on Philip Roth's *Portnoy's Complaint:*
"Philip Roth is a good writer, but I wouldn't want to shake hands with him."

Journalist Arthur Marshall on Barbara Cartland:
"A tireless purveyor of romance and now a gleaming telly-figure with a Niagara of jabber and the white and creamy look of an animated meringue."

Tom Volpe on Harold Robbins:
"He is able to turn an unplotted, unworkable manuscript into an unplotted and unworkable manuscript with a lot of sex."

"Jackie Collins is to writing what her sister Joan is to acting."

Campbell Grison

Clive James on Judith Krantz's *Princess Daisy:*
"As a work of art, it has the same status as a long conversation between two not very bright drunks."

Columnist Ellen Goodman on Danielle Steel's *Message from Nam:*
"I regard this novel as a work without any redeeming social value, unless it can be recycled as a cardboard box."

Agatha Christie on Agatha Christie:
"A sausage machine, a perfect sausage machine."

Dorothy Parker on *New Yorker* founding editor Harold Ross:
"His ignorance was an Empire State Building of ignorance. You had to admire it for its size."

"[Alexander Solzhenitsyn] is a bad novelist and a fool. The combination usually makes for great popularity in the U.S."
Gore Vidal

"[Arianna Stassinopoulos is a writer] so boring you fall asleep halfway through her name."
British author Alan Bennett

Julia Burchill wrote in *The Spectator*, about Camille Paglia:
"The *g* is silent—the only thing about her that is."

"[Writers:] schmucks with Underwoods."
Jack Warner

"An editor should have a pimp for a brother so he'd have someone to look up to."
Gene Fowler

"One should not be too severe on English novelists. They are the only relaxation of the intellectually unemployed."
Oscar Wilde

"It would be an advantage to the literary world if most writers stopped writing entirely."

Fran Lebowitz

"The road to hell is paved with works-in-progress."

Philip Roth

"All writers are vain, selfish, and lazy, and at the very bottom their motives are a mystery."

George Orwell

"Everywhere I go I'm asked if I think the university stifles writers. My opinion is that they don't stifle enough of them. There's many a best-seller that could have been prevented by a good teacher."

Flannery O'Connor

"One reason the human race has such a low opinion of itself is that it gets so much of its wisdom from writers."

Wilfrid Sheed

"Literature is mostly about having sex, and not much about having babies; life is the other way 'round."

David Lodge

"Having been unpopular in high school is not just cause for book publications."

Fran Lebowitz

"Authors are easy enough to get on with—if you are fond of children."

Michael Joseph

"There are no dull subjects. There are only dull writers."

H. L. Mencken

"Only a mediocre writer is always at his best."

W. Somerset Maugham

"The paperback is very interesting, but I find it will never replace a hardcover book—it makes a very poor doorstop."

Alfred Hitchcock

"I would sooner read a timetable or a catalogue than nothing at all. They are much more interesting than half the novels written."

W. Somerset Maugham

"Poets, like whores, are only hated by each other."

William Wycherley

"Some prose writers go from bad to verse."

Anonymous

"I gave up on poetry myself thirty years ago, when most of it began to read like coded messages passing between lonely aliens in a hostile world."

Russell Baker

"[Rod McKuen's] poetry is not even trash."

Karl Shapiro

John Cheever on Russian poet Yevgeny Yevtushenko: "An ego that can crack crystal at a distance of twenty feet."

"Poetry is what happens when an anxiety meets a technique."

Lawrence Durrell

"There is no money in poetry, but then there is no poetry in money, either."

Robert Graves

"All bad poetry springs from genuine feeling."

Oscar Wilde

"Editors used to be known by their authors; now some of them are known by their restaurants."

Robert Giroux

"Journalism is organized gossip."

Edward Eggleston

"Most rock journalism is people who can't write interviewing people who can't talk for people who can't read."

Frank Zappa

"They should give [gossip columnist Joyce Haber] open-heart surgery—and go in through the feet."

Julie Andrews

"No self-respecting dead fish would want to be wrapped in a Murdoch newspaper, let alone work for it."

George Royko

A writer once submitted a manuscript to Samuel Johnson, who read it and promptly wrote:
"Your manuscript is both good and original; but the part that is good is not original, and the part that is original is not good."

"If a young writer can refrain from writing, he shouldn't hesitate to do so."

André Gide

CRITICS

"A critic is a man who writes about things he doesn't like."

Anonymous

"Critics can't even make music by rubbing their back legs together."

Mel Brooks

"Critics? I love every bone in their heads."

Eugene O'Neill

"A critic is a legless man who teaches running."

Channing Pollock

"Having the critics praise you is like having the hangman say you've got a pretty neck."

Eli Wallach

"Those who can't—teach. And those who can't do either—review."

Burt Reynolds

"American critics are like American universities. They both have dull and half-dead faculties."

Edward Albee

"[Critics are] drooling, driveling, doleful, depressing, dropsical drips."

Sir Thomas Beecham

"Critics are the stupid who discuss the wise."

Anonymous

"Critics are like eunuchs in a harem: They know how it's done, they've seen it done every day, but they're unable to do it themselves."

Brendan Behan

"Don't pay attention to bad reviews. Today's newspaper is tomorrow's toilet paper."

Jack Warner

Movie director Josh Logan once said to Truman Capote: "Say anything you want about me, but you make fun of my picture and you'll regret it for the rest of your fat midget life."

John Simon on movie critic Rex Reed:
"Manifestly subliterate."

"Rex Reed is either at your feet or at your throat."
Ava Gardner

"You have to make important differences between critics and assassins. There are important differences between John Simon and Sirhan Sirhan. Sirhan Sirhan is in jail."
Rocco Landesman

"They released a big study about how bad movie theater popcorn is for you. In fact, we went to the movies last night. The popcorn came in three sizes: medium, large, and Roger Ebert's Tub of Death."

Jay Leno

"Any fool can criticize—and many of them do."
Cyril Garbett

"Pauline Kael is the Rambo of film critics . . . a demented bag lady."

Director Alan Parker

Gael Greene on restaurant critic Mimi Sheraton:
"I would trust her totally on cottage cheese."

"A drama critic is a man who leaves no turn unstoned."
George Bernard Shaw

"Critics are like mayors of New York; nobody really wants to like them."
Dore Schary

"A critic is a man who knows the way, but can't drive the car."
Kenneth Tynan

"A bad review is like baking a cake with all the best ingredients and having someone sit on it."
Danielle Steel

"Critics are probably more prone to clichés than fiction writers who pluck things out of the air."
Critic and screenwriter Penelope Gilliatt

"Honest criticism is hard to take, particularly from a relative, a friend, an acquaintance, or a stranger."
Franklin P. Jones

"Critics are a dissembling, dishonest, contemptible race of men. Asking a working writer what he feels about critics is like asking a lamppost what he feels about dogs."

John Osborne

SHOW BUSINESS

. . . .

"If you say a modern celebrity is an adulterer, a pervert, and a drug addict, all it means is that you've read his autobiography."

P. J. O'Rourke

Upon seeing the huge crowd attending Louis B. Mayer's funeral in 1957, Billy Wilder said ruefully, "Give the public what it wants and they'll show up."

"The reason so many people showed up at [Mayer's] funeral was because they wanted to make sure he was dead."

Samuel Goldwyn

"[L. B. Mayer] had the memory of an elephant and the hide of an elephant. The only difference is that elephants are vegetarians, and Mayer's diet was his fellow man."

Herman J. Mankiewicz

Jean Harlow had been mispronouncing Margot Asquith's name all evening. Finally, Asquith corrected her: "The *t* is silent, as in *Harlow*."

Bette Davis remarked on the death of a starlet:
"There goes the good time that was had by all."

"[Andy Warhol is] the only genius with an IQ of 60."
Gore Vidal

"Film directors are people too short to become actors."
Journalist Josh Greenfeld

"If my film makes one more person miserable, I've done my job."
Woody Allen

"Michael Apted directs *Blink* like a deli owner scraping mold off a cheese."
Critic John Powers

John Simon, reviewing *Jonathan Livingston Seagull*: "Seagulls, as the film stresses, subsist on garbage, and, I guess, you are what you eat."

"*My Dinner with André* is as boring as being alive."
Quentin Crisp

"[Francis Ford] Coppola couldn't piss in a pot."
Bob Hoskins

"Steven [Spielberg] always wanted to be a little boy when he grew up."
Rainer Werner Fassbinder

"I'm afraid [Martha Graham] is going to give birth to a cube."
Stark Young

"I'm as pure as the driven slush."
Tallulah Bankhead

Howard Dietz on Tallulah Bankhead:
"A day away from Tallulah is like a month in the country."

"Tallulah Bankhead is a marvelous female impersonator."
Anne Baxter

"Ed Sullivan will be around as long as someone else has talent."
Fred Allen

British satirist Jonathan Miller referred to David Frost as "the bubonic plagiarist."

"Richard Gere and Cindy Crawford—he's elastic and she's plastic."

Sandra Bernhard

On Gere and Crawford:
"His body's by Nautilus and her mind's by Mattel."

Sam Kinison

"Boy George is all England needs—another queen who can't dress."

Joan Rivers

"Radio is a bag of mediocrity where little men with carbon minds wallow in sluice of their own making."

Fred Allen

Linda Ellerbee on the show business aspect of news broadcasters:
"We call them Twinkies. You've seen them on television acting the news, modeling and fracturing the news while you wonder whether they've read the news—or if they've blow-dried their brains, too."

"You can learn more by watching *Let's Make a Deal* than you can by watching Walter Cronkite for a month."

Monty Hall

Walter Cronkite on Andy Rooney:
"We've all had the experience of listening to him talk until an idea comes along. I don't know how Andy can make 60 seconds on *60 Minutes* seem like 60 hours."

"Word has it that [Jimmy] Carter even said he would willingly bequeath President Reagan two things—Menachem Begin and Sam Donaldson. We'll take Begin, but Donaldson . . ."

> *Reagan press secretary*
> *Larry Speakes*

"Is Connie Chung a real journalist or just a reenactment of one?

> *Rolling Stone*

"Bryant Gumble's ego has applied for statehood. And if it's accepted, it will be the fifth largest."

> Today *show weatherman*
> *Willard Scott*

Russian poet Yevgeny Yevtushenko referred to Barbara Walters as "a hyena in syrup."

"If Geraldo Rivera is the first journalist in space, NASA can test weightlessness on weightlessness."

> *Anonymous*

"I once shook hands with Pat Boone and my whole right side sobered up."

Dean Martin

"Television—a medium. So called because it is neither rare nor well done."

Ernie Kovaks

"If vaudeville had died, television was the box they put it in."

Larry Gelbart

"Television—chewing gum for the eyes."

Frank Lloyd Wright

"*All* television is children's television."

Richard P. Adler

"Television is a device that permits people who haven't anything to do watch people who can't do anything."

Fred Allen

"Television has raised writing to a new low."

Samuel Goldwyn

" 'Dinner Theater,' a way of positively guaranteeing that both food and theater will be amateur and mediocre, which means unthreatening and therefore desirable."

Paul Fussell

Luchino Visconti on fellow director Michelangelo Antonioni: "It seems that boredom is one of the great discoveries of our time. If so, there's no question but that he must be considered a pioneer."

Film commentator Leslie Halliwell on Blake Edwards: "A man of many talents, all of them minor."

"Since Godard's films have nothing to say, we could perhaps have ninety minutes of silence instead of each of them."

John Simon

"Jane Fonda . . . is so obsessed with remaining inhumanly taut by working out ninety-two hours a day that it took her more than a decade to notice that she was married to a dweeb."

Dave Barry

"Good taste would likely have the same effect on Howard Stern that daylight has on Dracula."

Ted Koppel

ACTORS

"They shot too many pictures and not enough actors."
Walter Winchell

"You can pick out the actors by the glazed look that comes into their eyes when the conversation wanders away from themselves."
British actor Michael Wilding

"Don't ever forget what I'm going to tell you: Actors are crap."
John Ford

"The physical labor actors have to do wouldn't tax an embryo."
Neil Simon

When movie mogul Darryl F. Zanuck needed to defend himself for having had so many affairs, he hastened to point out, "Any of my indiscretions were with people, not actresses."

"An actor's a guy who, if you ain't talkin' about him, ain't listening."

Marlon Brando

Noël Coward was told that a certain actor had committed suicide by shooting his brains out. "He must have been a marvelous shot," Coward quipped.

Upon reading the script for *Private Lives,* in which she was to star, Gertrude Lawrence sent Noël Coward the following telegram:
"Nothing wrong that can't be fixed."
His reply: "Nothing to be fixed except your performance."

"Acting is like roller skating—once you know how to do it, it is neither stimulating nor exciting."

George Sanders

Walter Kerr on an anonymous actor:
"He had delusions of adequacy."

"Lillian Gish may be a charming person, but she is not Ophelia. She comes on stage as if she had been sent for to sew rings on the new curtains."

Mrs. Patrick Campbell

Actress Dame Margaret Kendal on Sarah Bernhardt: "A great actress, from the waist down."

"Scratch an actor, and you'll find an actress."

Dorothy Parker

"Every actor has a natural animosity toward every other actor, present or absent, living or dead."

Louise Brooks

"[Alfred Lunt] has his head in the clouds and his feet in the box office."

Noël Coward

Fanny Brice on Esther Williams: "Wet, she's a star. Dry, she ain't."

W. C. Fields on Mae West: "A plumber's idea of Cleopatra."

S. J. Perelman on Groucho Marx:
"The man was a major comedian, which is to say that he had the compassion of an icicle, the effrontery of a carnival shill, and the generosity of a pawnbroker."

"All I want to see is the horror picture to end all horror pictures. It should be called *Frankenstein Meets Mickey Rooney*. And I don't care how it comes out."

An anonymous MGM producer

"[Mickey Rooney's] favorite exercise is climbing tall people."

Phyllis Diller

"I never said all actors are cattle. What I said was all actors should be *treated* like cattle."

Alfred Hitchcock

When ingenue Mary Anderson asked Alfred Hitchcock which was her "best side," the director replied, "My dear, you're sitting on it."

"She's descended from a long line her mother listened to."

Gypsy Rose Lee, on a 1940s movie star

Alexander Woollcott told a boring young actor, "Excuse me, my leg has gone to sleep. Do you mind if I join it?"

Lionel Barrymore on Margaret O'Brien:
"If this child had been born in the Middle Ages, she'd have been burned as a witch."

Louise Brooks referred to child star Shirley Temple as "a swaggering, tough little slut."

Carl Sandburg on Gary Cooper:
"One of the most beloved illiterates this country has ever known."

King Vidor on Cooper:
"He's got a reputation as a great actor just by thinking hard about the next line."

"If Greta Garbo really wants to be alone, she should come to a performance of one of her films in Dublin."
An unnamed Irish critic

"[Otto Preminger] is a horrible man, phew! But who ever hears of him anymore? Is he dead?"
Dyan Cannon

"The nicest thing I can say about Frances Farmer is that she is unbearable."
William Wyler

"I thank God that neither I nor any member of my family will ever be so hard up that we have to work for Otto Preminger."

Lana Turner

"[Rita Hayworth was] the worst lay in the world—she was always drunk and never stopped eating."

Peter Lawford

"Bette [Davis] and I are very good friends. There's nothing I wouldn't say to her face—both of them."

Tallulah Bankhead, responding to allegations that Davis had impersonated her throughout All About Eve

"Miss Bankhead isn't well enough known nationally to warrant my imitating her."

Bette Davis

"Toward the end of her life [Joan Crawford] looked like a hungry insect magnified a million times—a praying mantis that had forgotten how to pray."

Quentin Crisp

Stanley Kauffmann on Vittorio De Sica:
"A fine actor, a polished hack, and a flabby whore—not necessarily in that order."

David Susskind on Tony Curtis:
"A passionate amoeba."

"[Marilyn Monroe] was good at playing abstract confusion in the same way that a midget is good at being short. . . . As far as talent goes, [she] was so minimally gifted as to be unemployable, and anyone who holds to the opinion that she was a great natural comic identifies himself immediately as a dunce."

Australian critic Clive James

"[Marilyn Monroe:] A broad with a big future behind her."

Constance Bennett

"I don't think [Marilyn Monroe] could act her way out of a paper script. She has no charm, delicacy, or taste. She is just an arrogant little tail-twitcher who learned to throw sex in your face."

American screenwriter Nunnally Johnson

Betty Friedan on Groucho:
"He's a male chauvinistic piglet."

"When they asked Jack Benny to do something for the Actors' Orphanage—he shot both his parents and moved in."

Bob Hope

"George [Burns], you're too old to get married again. Not only can't you cut the mustard, honey, you're too old to open the jar."

LaWanda Page

"[Clark Gable] is the kind of guy who, if you say, 'Hiya, Clark, how are yah?', is stuck for an answer."

Ava Gardner

David Niven on Jayne Mansfield:
"Miss United Dairies herself."

The *Detroit Free Press* on David Niven:
"We are privileged to see Mr. Samuel Goldwyn's latest 'discovery.' All we can say about this actor is that he is tall, dark, and not the slightest bit handsome."

"Miss Garland's figure resembles the giant-economy-size tube of toothpaste in girls' bathrooms: Squeezed intemperately at all points, it acquires a shape that defies definition by the most resourceful solid geometrician."

John Simon

"Zsa Zsa Gabor not only worships the Golden Calf—she barbecues it for lunch."

Oscar Levant

Elliott Gould on Jerry Lewis:
"This arrogant, sour, ceremonial, pious, chauvinistic ego-maniac."

"[Katharine Hepburn] ran the whole gamut of the emotions from A to B, and put some distance between herself and a more experienced colleague [Alison Skipworth] lest she catch some acting from her."

Dorothy Parker, at the first night of The Lake *in 1933*

"[Katharine Hepburn] has a cheekbone like a death's head allied to a manner as sinister and aggressive as crossbones."

James Agate

Upon the completion of the movie *A Bill of Divorcement*, an unpleasantly tense experience for all involved, Katharine Hepburn told John Barrymore, "Thank God, I don't have to act with you anymore." "I didn't realize you ever had, darling," Barrymore replied.

"[Paul Henreid] looks as if his idea of fun would be to find a cold damp grave and sit in it."

Richard Winnington

"[Marion Davies] has only two expressions—joy and indigestion."

Dorothy Parker

Walter Kerr on Ethel Merman in *Gypsy:*
"Brassy, brazen witch on a mortgaged broomstick, a steam-roller with cleats."

"The best time I had with Joan Crawford was when I pushed her down the stairs in *Whatever Happened to Baby Jane?*"
Bette Davis

"Overweight, overbosomed, overpaid, and under-talented, [Elizabeth Taylor] set the acting profession back a decade."
David Susskind

Kevin Kelly on the 1986 production of *Private Lives:*
"Elizabeth Taylor, sounding something like Minnie Mouse and weighted down to her ankles in comedic intent, keeps crashing against the trees while Richard Burton . . . slogs up and down oddly majestic molehills."

"Before [Burt Lancaster] can pick up an ashtray, he discusses his motivation for an hour or two. You want to say, 'Just pick up the ashtray, and shut up!' "
Jeanne Moreau

Oscar Levant on Audrey Hepburn:
"A walking X-ray."

"[Anthony Quinn] needs a personality transplant."
Pauline Kael

"Most of the time, [Marlon Brando] sounds like he has a mouth full of toilet paper."
Rex Reed

"A Steve McQueen performance just naturally lends itself to monotony. Steve doesn't bring much to the party."
Robert Mitchum

"[Steve McQueen's] features resembled a fossilized washrag."
Critic Alan Brien

Director Josh Logan found Lee Marvin extremely difficult to work with:
"Not since Attila the Hun swept across Europe leaving 500 years of total blackness has there been a man like Lee Marvin."

Dwight Macdonald on Doris Day:
"As wholesome as a bowl of cornflakes and at least as sexy."

"The only real talent Miss Day possesses is that of being absolutely sanitary: her personality untouched by human emotions, her brow unclouded by human thought, her form unsmudged by the slightest form of femininity."

John Simon

Ava Gardner on Frank Sinatra's marriage to Mia Farrow: "Hah! I always knew Frank would end up in bed with a boy!"

Don Rickles on Frank Sinatra: "When you enter a room, you have to kiss his ring. I don't mind, but he has it in his back pocket."

British producer Roy Boulting on Peter Sellers: "As a man he was abject, probably his own worst enemy, although there was plenty of competition."

"While I was very fond of Paul Newman and Peter Sellers, I'd have to say that I would rather kiss a tree trunk."

Elke Sommer

Film buff Harry Medved on Dean Martin's performance in *The Ambushers*: "Martin's acting is so inept that even his impersonation of a lush seems unconvincing."

"At one point, a hot-blooded gang leader shows his contempt for [Pat] Boone by striking him and spitting in his face (perhaps he has seen some of Boone's earlier screen work, such as *April Love* or *All Hands on Deck*)."

Critics Harry and Michael Medved,
on Boone's performance in
The Cross and the Switchblade

Jane Fonda on Laurence Harvey, her costar in *A Walk on the Wild Side:*
"Acting with Harvey is like acting by yourself—only worse."

Laurence Harvey to his costar Capucine during the filming of *A Walk on the Wild Side:*
"If you were more of a woman, I would be more of a man. Kissing you is like kissing the side of a beer bottle."

Pauline Kael on Peter Fonda:
"It looks as if somehow, on the set of *The Grapes of Wrath,* John Carradine and Henry Fonda had mated."

"Dustin Hoffman is the luckiest Jewish midget that ever lived."

Screenwriter Martin Rackin

"[Daryl Hannah] looks like a linebacker in a Lorelei wig."
John Simon

When Dennis Hopper directed *Hot Spot,* he explained why Don Johnson was cast as the lead:
"He's an ass. He was perfect for the part. He was an amoral drifter who will blackmail you and take everything he can from you. And you better watch yourself because when you turn your back, he might screw your wife."

Margot Kernan on Woody Allen in 1984:
"His Krafft is Ebing."

"I still don't believe that Raquel Welch exists. She has been manufactured by the media merely to preserve the sexless plasticity of sex objects for the masses."
Andrew Sarris

"One of [Raquel Welch's] major talents is the ability to stand up on stage without pitching over."
Critic Marvin Kitman

Mr. Blackwell, compiler of the "worst-dressed" lists, on Cher:
"A bag of tattooed bones in a sequined slingshot."

John Simon on Liza Minnelli:
"That turnipy nose overhanging a forward-gaping mouth and hastily retreating chin, that bulbous cranium with eyes as big (and as inexpressive) as saucers. . . ."

"Sandy Dennis has made an acting style out of postnasal drip."

Pauline Kael

"[Ann-Margret] does most of her acting inside of her mouth."

Pauline Kael

John Simon on Maximilian Schell:
"If a fetchingly cleft chin can be called a performance, Schell can be said to act."

"Since making her debut as Lakey the Lesbian in the film version of Mary McCarthy's *The Group,* Ms. Bergen has displayed the same emotional range and dramatic intensity as her father's dummy, Charlie McCarthy."

Critics Harry and Michael Medved

"Shirley MacLaine's the sort of liberal that if she found out who she was going to be in her next life, she'd make a will and leave all the money to herself."

Director Colin Higgins

Truman Capote on Meryl Streep:
"Oh God! She looks like a chicken."

"[Meryl Streep] seemed like a frozen, boring blonde, with ice water in her veins; from the Grace Kelly/Tippi Hedren School of Dramatic Art."

Rex Reed

Diane Keaton has "an acting style that's really a nervous breakdown in slow motion."

John Simon

"In real life, Diane Keaton believes in God. But she also believes that the radio works because there are tiny people inside it."

Woody Allen

"[Bette Midler] is not a bad person, but stupid in terms of gray matter. I mean, I like her, but I like my dog, too."

James Caan

"Joan Collins's career is a testimony to menopausal chic."

Erica Jong

"[Joan Collins] looks like she combs her hair with an egg-beater."

Louella Parsons

Christopher Plummer on his *Sound of Music* costar Julie Andrews:
"Working with her is like being hit over the head with a valentine."

"[Barbra Streisand] looks like a cross between an aardvark and an albino rat surmounted by a platinum-coated horse bun. . . . [Streisand has] a horse face centering on a nose that looks like Brancusi's *Rooster* cast in liverwurst."
John Simon

Katharine Hepburn on Sharon Stone:
"It's a new low for actresses when you have to wonder what's between her ears instead of her legs."

"When it comes to acting, Joan Rivers has the range of a wart."
Stewart Klein

"[Sylvester Stallone's] big asset: a face that would look well upon a three-toed sloth. If not the Incredible, Stallone is at least the most Improbable Hulk."
British critic Russell Davies

"[Sylvester Stallone's] diction (always bad) is now incomprehensible, as if his ego has grown so big that it now fills his mouth like a cup of mashed potatoes."
John Powers

"I don't get why anyone takes [Steven Seagal] seriously. With his soft chin, black-shirted paunch, and ponytail the size of a chihuahua's penis, Seagal looks more like a schnorrer at a Hollywood party than like the toughest man in creation."

John Powers

"[Anjelica Houston] has the face of an exhausted gnu, the voice of an unstrung tennis racket, and a figure of no describable shape."

John Simon

"After Arnold Schwarzenegger, Dolph Lundgren is a bit of a disappointment. At least Arnold looks like he comes supplied with batteries."

Adam Mars-Jones

"Kevin Costner is like Oakland: There is no there there."

Marcello Mastroianni

"How does . . . Francis Ford Coppola, one of the greatest filmmakers of our time, see Keanu Reeves's work, see what we've all seen, and say, 'That's what I want in my movie?' "

Charlie Sheen

"[Bo Derek] turned down the role of Helen Keller because she couldn't remember the lines."

Joan Rivers

"Disney, of course, has the best casting. If he doesn't like an actor, he just tears him up."

Alfred Hitchcock

"[Farrah Fawcett] is uniquely suited to play a woman of limited intelligence."

Critics Harry and Michael Medved

ART AND ARTISTS

. . . .

"If the old masters had labeled their fruit, one wouldn't be so likely to mistake pears for turnips."

Mark Twain

Auguste Renoir on Leonardo da Vinci:
"He bores me. He ought to have stuck to his flying machines."

Diarist Marie Bashkirtseff wrote, "Leonardo da Vinci did everything and did nothing very well."

American critic Kenyon Cox referred to Paul Gauguin in 1913 as "a decorator tainted with insanity."

"[Paul Klee's] pictures seem to resemble, not pictures, but a sample book of patterns of linoleum."

British critic Cyril Asquith

"I wouldn't have that [painting] hanging in my home. It would be like living with a gas leak."

Edith Evans

"[Claude Monet was] a skillful but short-lived decorator."

Edgar Degas

"Just explain to Monsieur Renoir that the torso of a woman is not a mass of decomposing flesh, its green and violet spots indicating the state of complete putrefaction of a corpse."

Critic Albert Wolff

French writer Jules Renard on Toulouse-Lautrec:
"A tiny Vulcan with pince-nez, a little twin-pounced bag in which he stuck his poor legs."

Ernest Hemingway on British artist Wyndham Lewis:
"I don't think I have ever seen a nastier looking man. Under the black hat, when I had first seen them, the eyes had been those of an unsuccessful rapist."

"Mr. Lewis's pictures appeared . . . to have been painted by a mailed fist in a cotton glove."

Dame Edith Sitwell

"The naked truth about me is to the naked truth about Salvador Dalí as an old ukelele in the attic is to a piano in a tree, and I mean a piano with breasts."

James Thurber

Australian art critic Robert Hughes had this to say about the work of American artist Jeff Koons:
"The last bit of methane left in the intestine of the dead cow that is post-modernism."

"Modern art is like trying to follow the plot in alphabet soup."

Anonymous

"Art for art's sake makes no more sense than gin for gin's sake."

W. Somerset Maugham

"Performance art is created by thin young men and usually consists of dancerly women taking their clothes off, putting on masks, and dumping blood on each other while a sound track screeches out machinery noises."

Ian Shoales

"Abstract art: a product of the untalented sold by the unprincipled to the utterly bewildered."

Al Capp

"If more than ten percent of the population likes a painting it should be burned, for it must be bad."

George Bernard Shaw

"Bad artists always admire each other's work."

Oscar Wilde

MUSIC AND MUSICIANS

. . . .

"Of all noises, I think music is the least disagreeable."

Samuel Johnson

"[George Frideric Handel was] a tub of pork and beer."

Hector Berlioz

"Beethoven always sounds like the upsetting of bags—with here and there a dropped hammer."

John Ruskin

Beethoven to a fellow composer:
"I liked your opera. I think I will set it to music."

"The Detroit String Quartet played Brahms last night. Brahms lost."

Bennett Cerf

"Is Wagner a human being at all? Is he not rather a disease? He contaminates everything he touches—he has made music sick. I postulate this viewpoint: Wagner's art is diseased."

Friedrich Nietzsche

"The music of Wagner imposes mental tortures that only algebra has a right to inflict."

French critic Paul de Saint-Victor

"Wagner writes like an intoxified pig."

British critic George T. Strong

"Wagner's music is better than it sounds."

Mark Twain

"Liszt's orchestral music is an insult to art. It is gaudy musical harlotry, savage and incoherent bellowings."

An anonymous critic

"I can compare *Le Carnaval romain* by [Hector] Berlioz to nothing but the caperings and gibberings of a big baboon, over-excited by a dose of alcoholic stimulus."

George T. Strong

"Saint-Saëns has informed a delighted public that since the war began he has composed music for the stage and a piece for the trombone. If he'd been making shell cases instead, it might have been all the better for music."

Maurice Ravel

Critic Edward Robinson on Ravel's *Boléro:*
"The most insolent monstrosity ever perpetrated in the story of music. From the beginning to the end of its 339 measures it is simply the incredible repetition of the same rhythm and above all it is the blatant recurrence of an overwhelmingly vulgar cabaret tune that is little removed from the wail of an obstreperous back-alley cat."

"The leader of cacophonists is Arnold Schoenberg. He learned a lesson from militant suffragettes. He was ignored till he began to smash the parlor furniture, throw bombs, and hitch together ten pianolas, all playing different tunes, whereupon everybody began to talk about him. In Schoenberg's later works, all the laws of construction, observed by the masters from Bach to Wagner, are ignored, insulted, trampled upon. The statue of Venus, the Goddess of Beauty, is knocked from its pedestal and replaced by the stone image of the Goddess of Ugliness, with the hideous features of a Hottentot hag."

American critic Henry T. Finck

"[Schoenberg] would be better off shoveling snow."

Richard Strauss

"Stravinsky looks like a man who was potty-trained too early and that music proves it as far as I am concerned."

British writer Russell Hoban,
in Turtle Diary

"[Dmitri] Shostakovich is without doubt the foremost composer of pornographic music in the history of art. He has accomplished the feat of penning passages which, in their faithful portrayal of what is going on, become obscene. The whole scene is little better than a glorification of the sort of stuff that filthy pencils write on lavatory walls."

American critic W. J. Henderson

"Listening to the Fifth Symphony of Ralph Vaughan Williams is like staring at a cow for forty-five minutes."

Aaron Copland

"When an opera singer sings her head off, she usually improves her appearance."

Victor Borge

"Of all the noises known to man, opera is the most expensive."

Voltaire

"Going to the opera, like getting drunk, is a sin that carries its own punishment with it and that a very severe one."

Hannah More

"How wonderful opera would be if there were no singers."

Gioacchino Rossini

"Rossini would have been a great composer if his teacher had spanked him enough on the backside."

Ludwig van Beethoven

"I occasionally play works by contemporary composers and for two reasons. First, to discourage the composer from writing any more, and second, to remind myself how much I appreciate Beethoven."

Jascha Heifetz

"There are more bad musicians than there is bad music."

Isaac Stern

"If you want to please only the critics, don't play too loud, too soft, too fast, too slow."

Arturo Toscanini

"Harpists spend ninety percent of their lives tuning their harps and ten percent playing out of tune."

Igor Stravinsky

"Classical music is music written by famous dead foreigners."

Arlene Heath

"Composers shouldn't think too much—it interferes with their plagiarism."

Howard Dietz

"People are wrong when they say that the opera isn't what it used to be. It *is* what it used to be. That's what's wrong with it."

Noël Coward

T. S. Eliot on *My Fair Lady:*
"I must say [George] Bernard Shaw is greatly improved by music."

Bernard Levin, writing in the *Daily Express* about Rodgers and Hammerstein's *Flower Drum Song:*
"An American musical so bad at times I longed for the boy-meets-tractor theme of Soviet drama."

Noël Coward on *Camelot:*
"It's like *Parsifal* without the jokes."

John Simon on the film of *Camelot:*
"This film is the Platonic idea of boredom, roughly comparable to reading a three-volume novel in a language of which one knows only the alphabet."

Clive Barnes on *Oh! Calcutta!:*
"The sort of show that gives pornography a bad name."

Stanley Kauffmann on *Jesus Christ Superstar:*
"It will flow on, if only at a syrup's pace. Religion and athe-
ism will both survive it."

Michael Billington, writing in *The Guardian* about a revival
of *Godspell:*
"*Godspell* is back. . . . For those who missed it the first time,
this is your golden opportunity: You can miss it again."

Ian Shoales on the musical *Annie:*
"I had to hit myself on the head afterward with a small
hammer to get that stupid 'Tomorrow' song out of my
head."

The New York Times on *Starlight Express:*
"A confusing jamboree of piercing noise, routine roller-
skating, misogyny, and Orwellian special effects, *Starlight
Express* is the perfect gift for the kid who has everything
except parents."

The New York Times on *Phantom of the Opera:*
"Mr. [Andrew] Lloyd Webber has again written a score so ge-
neric that most of the songs could be reordered and redistrib-
uted among the characters (indeed, among other Lloyd Webber
musicals) without altering the show's story or meaning."

Reviewing Elvis Presley's movie *Love Me Tender* in 1956, *Time* magazine wrote:
"Is it a sausage? It is certainly smooth and damp-looking, but whoever heard of a 172-lb. sausage six feet tall?"

"[Johnnie Ray] was the Jayne Mansfield of pop, totally dumb and unautonomous and out of control with no redeeming merit whatsoever—no voice, no songs, no music."

British critic Julie Burchill

"Rock music is the most brutal, ugly, vicious form of expression . . . sly, lewd—in plain fact, dirty . . . a rancid-smelling aphrodisiac . . . martial music of every delinquent on the face of the earth."

Frank Sinatra

"[Frankie Laine's] approach to the microphone is that of an accused man pleading with a hostile jury."

Kenneth Tynan

After Anita Bryant's anti-gay crusade got under way, she told the media she feared retribution. Gore Vidal:
"As to Anita's fear that she'll be assassinated? The only people who might shoot Anita Bryant are music lovers."

"You don't have to be Jewish to enjoy [Allen Sherman's] 'Hello Muddah, Hello Faddah'; all you need is extremely poor taste."

John Simon

"Mick Jagger is about as sexy as a pissing toad."
Truman Capote

British critic Laura Lee Davies on Tina Turner:
"All legs and hair with a mouth that could swallow the whole stadium and the hot dog stand."

Q: "What has 300 legs and 7 teeth?"
A: "The front row at a Willie Nelson concert."
Playboy

"[Rod Stewart] has an attractive voice and a highly unattractive bottom. In his concert performances, he now spends more time wagging the latter than exercising the former, thereby conforming to the established pattern by which popular entertainers fall prey to the delusion that the public loves them for themselves, and not for their work."
Australian critic Clive James

"[Leonard Cohen] gives you the feeling that your dog just died."
Q *magazine*

Judy Tenuta on Madonna:
"She's like a breast with a boom box."

"[Judd] Nelson gives a performance with flair: His eyes flare, his nostrils flare, his hair—if such a thing is possible—flares. His tonsils may have been flaring too, but at least you can't see them."

Writer Tom Shales

"Def Leppard . . . to me they're the George Bush of rock 'n roll."

Jim Steinman

"[Billy Ray] Cyrus helped turn country music into beef jerky: short on funk, low on nutrition, and punishing to the digestion. . . . Cyrus took his choreography from Chippendales and his musical standards from the Chipmunks."

Time *magazine*

"If white bread could sing, it would sound like Olivia Newton-John."

Anonymous

"Somebody should clip Sting around the head and tell him to stop singing in that ridiculous Jamaican accent."

Elvis Costello

"[Elvis Costello] looks like Buddy Holly after drinking a can of STP Oil Treatment."

Music writer Dave Marsh

Mark Coleman on Duran Duran:
"A baroque art-rock bubblegum broadcast on a frequency understood only by female teenagers and bred field mice."

A pseudonymous columnist in the London *Daily Mail* wrote the following about Liberace's arrival in London in 1956: "[Liberace] reeks of emetic language that can only make grown men long for a quiet corner, an aspidistra, a hand-kerchief, and the old heave-ho. Without doubt, he is the biggest sentimental vomit of all time."

Australian critic Clive James wrote in the *Observer,* of Charles Aznavour, "He's so worn by experience he's got bags under his head."

"The Beatles are not merely awful, I would consider it sacrilegious to say anything less than that they are godawful. They are so unbelievably horrible, so appallingly unmusical, so dogmatically insensitive to the magic of art, that they qualify as crowned heads of anti-music, even as the imposter popes went down in history as anti-popes."

William F. Buckley

"Paul McCartney has become the oldest living cute boy in the world."

Anna Quindlen

"To hear Tom Jones sing Sinatra's 'My Way' is roughly akin to watching Tab Hunter play King Lear. Mr. Jones is, in the words of his own hit, not unusual . . . at least not as a singer; as a sex symbol he is nothing short of inexplicable."
Sheridan Morley

"Michael Jackson's album was only called 'Bad' because there wasn't enough room on the sleeve for 'Pathetic.' "
The Artist Formerly Known as Prince

"Michael Jackson—he started life as a black man; now he's a white girl."
Comedian Mary Frances Connelly

"[The Artist Formerly Known as Prince] looks like a dwarf who's been dipped in a bucket of pubic hair."
Boy George

FOOD

. . . .

"The food in Yugoslavia is fine if you like pork tartare."
Ed Begley Jr.

"Poland is now a totally independent nation, and it has managed to greatly improve its lifestyle thanks to the introduction of modern Western conveniences, such as food."
Dave Barry

"England has forty-two religions and only two sauces."
Voltaire

An anonymous French chef on English cooking:
"You just put things in hot water and take them out again after a while."

"England is the only country in the world where the food is more dangerous than sex. I mean, a hard cheese will kill you, but a soft cheese will kill you in *seconds*."

Jackie Mason

"Japanese food is very pretty and undoubtedly a suitable cuisine in Japan, which is largely populated by people of below average size."

Fran Lebowitz

"Oats: A grain, which in England is generally given to horses, but in Scotland supports the people."

Samuel Johnson

"[Iceberg lettuce:] The polyester of greens."

John Waters

"Most turkeys taste better the day after [Thanksgiving]; my mother's tasted better the day before."

Rita Rudner

"We're doing something a little different this year at Thanksgiving. Instead of a turkey, we're having a swan. You get more stuffing."

George Carlin

"I don't like food that's too carefully arranged; it makes me think that [the chef is] spending too much time arranging and not enough time cooking. If I wanted a picture I'd buy a painting."

Andy Rooney

"I'm frightened of eggs, worse than frightened, they revolt me. That white round thing without any holes . . . have you ever seen anything more revolting than an egg yolk breaking and spilling its yellow liquid? Blood is jolly, red. But egg yolk is yellow, revolting. I've never tasted it."

Alfred Hitchcock

"The French-fried potato has become an inescapable horror in almost every public eating place in the country. 'French fries,' say the menus, but they are not French fries any longer. They are a furry-textured substance with the taste of plastic wood."

Russell Baker

"A gourmet restaurant in Cincinnati is one where you leave the tray on the table after you eat."

Anonymous

"Do you know on this one block you can buy croissants in five different places? There's one store called Bonjour Croissant. It makes me want to go to Paris and open a store called Hello Toast."

Fran Lebowitz

"Most vegetarians look so much like the food they eat that they can be classified as cannibals."

Finley Peter Dunne

"They served haggis at the last dinner I attended. I didn't know whether to kick it or eat it. Having eaten it, I wished I'd have kicked it."

Stuart Turner

"[A fork is] an instrument used chiefly for the purpose of putting dead animals into the mouth."

Ambrose Bierce

"Only a dog or a Frenchman walks after he has eaten."

French dictum

"When those waiters ask me if I want some fresh-ground pepper, I ask if they have any aged pepper."

Andy Rooney

"We lived for days on nothing but food and water."

W. C. Fields

"I will not eat oysters. I want my food dead—not sick, not wounded—dead."

Woody Allen

Henry Beard on Chinese food:
"You do not sew with a fork and I see no reason why you should eat with knitting needles."

"The trouble with eating Italian food is that five or six days later you're hungry again."

George Miller

Henny Youngman on seafood restaurants:
"The catch of the day was hepatitis."

"We were taken to a fast-food café, where our order was fed into a computer. Our hamburgers, made from the flesh of chemically impregnated cattle, had been broiled over counterfeit charcoal, placed between slices of artificially flavored cardboard, and served to us by recycled juvenile delinquents."

Jean-Michel Chapereau

"I refuse to spend my life worrying about what I eat. There is no pleasure worth forgoing just for an extra three years in the geriatric ward."

John Mortimer

"The average cooking in the average hotel for the average Englishman explains to a large extent the English bleakness and taciturnity. Nobody can beam and warble while chewing pressed beef smeared with diabolical mustard. Nobody can exult aloud while ungluing from his teeth a quivering tapioca pudding."

Karel Čapek

"The burger was horrid, thin and bitty like a Pekingese's tongue."

Craig Brown

Carol Cutler on pâté:
"Nothing more than a French meat loaf that's had a couple of cocktails."

"I understand the big food companies are developing a tearless onion. I think they can do it—after all, they've already given us tasteless bread."

Robert Orben

"For our anniversary my wife wanted to go someplace she's never been before. So I took her to the kitchen."

Henny Youngman

"One of the disadvantages of wine is that it makes a man mistake words for thoughts."

Samuel Johnson

"Never eat Chinese food in Oklahoma."

Bryan Miller

"In Mexico we have a word for sushi: bait."

José Simon

"Large, naked, raw carrots are acceptable as food only to those who live in hutches eagerly awaiting Easter."

Fran Lebowitz

Peter Burns on vegetarianism:
"You are what you eat, and who wants to be a lettuce?"

"I have known many meat eaters to be far more nonviolent than vegetarians."

Mahatma Gandhi

"Vegetarians have wicked, shifty eyes and laugh in a cold, calculating manner. They pinch little children, steal stamps, drink water, favor beards."

J. B. Morton

"Health food may be good for the conscience, but Oreos taste a hell of a lot better."

Robert Redford

"Desserts remain for a moment or two in your mouth and for the rest of your life on your hips."

Peg Bracken

"Gluttony is not a secret vice."

Orson Welles

NATIONS

" 'My country right or wrong' is like saying, 'My mother drunk or sober.' "

G. K. Chesterton

"There have been many definitions of hell, but for the English the best definition is that it is the place where the Germans are the police, the Swedish are the comedians, the Italians are the defense force, Frenchmen dig the roads, the Belgians are the pop singers, the Spanish run the railways, the Turks cook the food, the Irish are the waiters, the Greeks run the government, and the common language is Dutch."

David Frost and Anthony Jay

"Frustrate a Frenchman, he will drink himself to death; an Irishman, he will die of angry hypertension; a Dane, he will shoot himself; an American, he will get drunk, shoot you, then establish a million-dollar aid program for your relatives. Then he will die of an ulcer."

S. A. Rudin

"Realizing that they will never be a world power, the Cypriots have decided to be a world nuisance."

George Mikes

"The Greeks—dirty and impoverished descendants of a bunch of la-di-da fruit salads who invented democracy and then forgot how to use it while walking around dressed up like girls."

P. J. O'Rourke

"The Holy Roman Empire was neither holy, nor Roman, nor an Empire."

Voltaire

"Italian devotion and German fasting have no meaning."

Danish saying

"India is an abstraction. . . . India is a geographical term. It is no more a united nation than the Equator."

Winston Churchill

"[Russia is] probably the most boring country in the history of nations."

Norman Mailer

"Russia scares me. The people on the buses are so serious they look like they're going to the electric chair."

Muhammad Ali

"There are few virtues which the Poles do not possess and there are few errors they have ever avoided."

Winston Churchill

"To live in Australia permanently is rather like going to a party and dancing all night with one's mother."

Barry Humphries

"You don't say 'Cheers' when you drink a cup of tea in the bush; you say, 'Christ, the flies!' "

Prince Charles

Clement Freud's impression of New Zealand:
"I find it hard to say, because when I was there it seemed to be shut."

"The Swedes have their medical expenses taken care of, all of their welfare costs paid for, their rent subsidized, and so much is done for them, that if they lose their car keys they promptly commit suicide."

Godfrey Cambridge

"German is the most extravagantly ugly language—it sounds like someone using a sick bag on a 747."

Willy Rushton

"One thing I will say for the Germans, they are always perfectly willing to give somebody else's land to somebody else."

Will Rogers

"I speak Spanish to God, Italian to women, French to men, and German to my horse."

Holy Roman emperor Charles V

"German is a language which was developed solely to afford the speaker the opportunity to spit at strangers under the guise of polite conversation."

National Lampoon

"The German lies as soon as he becomes polite."

German dictum

"How much disgruntled heaviness, lameness, dampness, how much beer is there in the German intelligence."

Friedrich Nietzsche

"The German may be as big as a poplar tree, but he is as stupid as a bean."

Polish saying

"The German may be a good fellow, but it's better to hang him just the same."

Russian saying

"Whenever the literary German dives into a sentence, that is the last you are going to see of him till he emerges on the other side of the Atlantic with his verb in his mouth."
Mark Twain

"I look upon Switzerland as an inferior sort of Scotland."
Sydney Smith

"Switzerland is a cursed, selfish, swinish country of brutes, placed in the most romantic region of the world."
Lord Byron

"Since both [Switzerland's] national products, snow and chocolate, melt, the cuckoo clock was invented solely in order to give tourists something solid to remember it by."
British humorist Alan Coren

"The Swiss are a neat and industrious people, none of whom is under seventy-five years of age. They make cheeses, milk chocolate, and watches, all of which, when you come right down to it, are fairly unnecessary."
Dorothy Parker

"France is a dog-hole."

William Shakespeare,
in All's Well That Ends Well

"[The French are] Germans with good food."
Fran Lebowitz

"The friendship of the French is like their wine, exquisite but of short duration."
German saying

"The French don't say what they mean, don't read as they write, and don't sing according to the notes."
Italian saying

"Have the Frenchman for thy friend, not for thy neighbor."
Byzantine emperor Nicephorus I

"The ignorance of French society gives one a rough sense of the infinite."
French writer Joseph Ernest Renan

"The Italians are wise before the act, the Germans in the act, the French after the act."
European saying

"Life can never be entirely dull to an American. When he has nothing else to do he can always spend a few years trying to discover who his grandfather was."
Paul Bourget

"The French are sawed-off sissies who eat snails and slugs and cheese that smells like people's feet. Utter cowards who force their own children to drink wine, they gibber like baboons even when you try to speak to them in their own wimpy language."

P. J. O'Rourke

"Frenchmen resemble apes, who, climbing up a tree from branch to branch, never cease going till they come to the highest branch, and there they show their bare behinds."

Michel Eyquem de Montaigne

"Nobody can simply bring together a country that has 365 kinds of cheeses."

Charles de Gaulle

"If you're going to Paris you would do well to remember this: No matter how politely or distinctly you ask a Parisian a question, he will persist in answering you in French."

Fran Lebowitz

"France is a country where the money falls apart in your hands and you can't tear the toilet paper."

Billy Wilder

"One of the problems that Americans have with the French is that Americans think, before they go to France, that French people are basically like Maurice Chevalier. . . . So they go to France expecting to hear someone say, 'Sank heaven for leetle girls,' and instead they find some really sullen bureaucrat saying, 'Grandmoser's maiden name?' and they get irritated."

Calvin Trillin

"The trouble with Ireland is that it's a country full of genius, but with absolutely no talent."

Hugh Leonard

"The Irish are a fair people—they never speak well of one another."

Samuel Johnson

"Put an Irishman on the spit, and you can always get another Irishman to turn him."

George Bernard Shaw

"Give an Irishman lager for a month, and he's a dead man. An Irishman is lined with copper, and the beer corrodes it. But whiskey polishes the copper and is the saving of him."

Mark Twain

"Italy, at least, has two things to balance its miserable poverty and mismanagement: a lively intellectual movement and a good climate. Ireland is Italy without these two."

James Joyce

"I showed my appreciation of my native land in the usual Irish way by getting out of it as soon as I possibly could."

George Bernard Shaw

"The Koreans have been called 'The Irish of the East,' but this is an insult to the Irish."

James Kirkup

"I have been trying all my life to like Scotchmen, and am obligated to desist from the experiment in despair."

Charles Lamb

Dylan Thomas on Wales:
"The land of my fathers. My fathers can have it."

"England is a nation of shopkeepers."

Napoleon Bonaparte

"The English think soap is civilization."

Heinrich von Treitschke

"Britain is the only country in the world where being 'too clever by half' is an insult."

A. A. Gill

"The English never smash in a face. They merely refrain from asking it to dinner."

Margaret Halsey

"The English have an extraordinary ability for flying into a great calm."

Alexander Woollcott

"The English think incompetence is the same thing as sincerity."

Quentin Crisp

"[The English are] sheep with a nasty side."

Cyril Connolly

"The people of England are never so happy as when you tell them they are ruined."

Arthur Murray

"I did a picture in England once and it was so cold I almost got married."

Shelley Winters

"Silence can be defined as conversation with an Englishman."

Heinrich Heine

"When it's three o'clock in New York, it's still 1938 in London."

Bette Midler

"In London, they don't like you if you're still alive."

Harvey Fierstein

"What a pity it is that we have no amusements in England but vice and religion."

Sydney Smith

"Curse the blasted, jelly-boned swines, the slimy, the belly-wriggling invertebrates, the miserable sodding rotters, the flaming sods, the sniveling, dribbling, palsied, pulseless lot that make up England. They've got white of egg in their veins, and their spunk is that watery it's a marvel they can breed. They can nothing but frogspawn the gibberers. Why, why, why was I born an Englishman?"

D. H. Lawrence, after a publisher rejected his Sons and Lovers *in 1912*

"The most dangerous thing in the world is to make a friend of an Englishman, because he'll come sleep in your closet rather than spend ten shillings on a hotel."

Truman Capote

"Continental people have a sex life; the English have hot water bottles."

George Mikes

"The English instinctively admire any man who has no talent and is modest about it."

James Agate

"In America, only the successful writer is important. In France, all writers are important. In England, no writer is important. And in Australia, you have to explain what a writer is."

Geoffrey Cottrell

"[Americans'] demeanor is invariably morose, sullen, clown-ish, and repulsive. I should think there is not, on the face of the earth, a people so entirely destitute of humor, vivacity, or the capacity of enjoyment."

Charles Dickens

"There is nothing the matter with Americans except their ideals. The real American is all right; it is the ideal American who is all wrong."

G. K. Chesterton

"No one can be as calculatedly rude as the British, which amazes Americans, who do not understand studied insult and can only offer abuse as a substitute."

Paul Gallico

"America is the only nation in history which miraculously has gone from barbarism to degeneration without the usual interval of civilization."

Georges Clemenceau

"Of course, America had often been discovered before Columbus, but it had always been hushed up."

Oscar Wilde

"In America, sex is an obsession. In other parts of the world, it is a fact."

Marlene Dietrich

"The American male doesn't mature until he has exhausted all other possibilities."

Wilfred Sheed

"The Americans, like the English, probably make love worse than any other race."

Walt Whitman

"America is a large, friendly dog in a very small room. Every time it wags its tail, it knocks over a chair."

Arnold Toynbee

"The trouble with America is that there are far too many wide-open spaces surrounded by teeth."

Charles Luckman

"America is a mistake—a giant mistake!"

Sigmund Freud

"The American political system is like fast food—mushy, insipid, made out of disgusting parts of things, and everybody wants some."

P. J. O'Rourke

"The United States is a nation of laws: badly written and randomly enforced."

Frank Zappa

"America is the greatest of opportunities and the worst of influences."

George Santayana

"Americans are broad-minded people. They'll accept the fact that a person can be an alcoholic, a dope fiend, and a wife-beater, and even a newspaperman, but if a man doesn't drive, there's something wrong with him."

Art Buchwald

"America is one of the finest countries anyone ever stole."

Bobcat Goldthwaite

"The Americans don't really understand what's going on in Bosnia. To them, it's the unspellables killing the unpronounceables."

P. J. O'Rourke

"Americans will put up with anything provided it doesn't block traffic."

Dan Rather

"Americans are people who laugh at African witch doctors and spend 100 million dollars on fake reducing systems."

L. L. Levinson

"If you're going to America, bring your own food."

Fran Lebowitz

"If you surveyed a hundred typical middle-aged Americans, I bet you'd find that only two of them could tell you their blood types, but every last one of them would know the theme song from *The Beverly Hillbillies*."

Dave Barry

"America [is] just a nation of two hundred million used car salesmen with all the money we need to buy guns and no qualms about killing anybody else in the world who tries to make us uncomfortable."

Hunter S. Thompson

"Canada is useful only to provide me with furs."

Madame de Pompadour

"Canada is a country whose main exports are hockey players and cold fronts. Our main imports are baseball players and acid rain."

Pierre Trudeau

"In any world menu, Canada must be considered the vichyssoise of nations. It's cold, half-French, and difficult to stir."

Stuart Keate

"Canadians are generally indistinguishable from Americans, and the surest way of telling the two apart is to make the observation to a Canadian."

Richard Staines

"Canada is a country so square that even the female impersonators are women."

Richard Benner

"Very little is known of the Canadian country since it is rarely visited by anyone but the queen and illiterate sport fishermen."

P. J. O'Rourke

AMERICAN STATES

. . . .

"California's a wonderful place to live—if you happen to be
an orange."

Fred Allen

"In California, you lose a point off your I.Q. every year."

Truman Capote

"Californians invented the concept of lifestyle. This alone
warrants their doom."

Don DeLillo

"Who would want to live in a place where the only cultural
advantage is that you can turn right on a red light?"

Woody Allen,
commenting on California in Annie Hall

"Almost anything that's fun is going to be ruined sooner or later by people from California."

Calvin Trillin

"There's nothing wrong with southern California that a rise in the ocean level wouldn't cure."

Ross Macdonald

"In California, everyone goes to a therapist, is a therapist, or is a therapist going to a therapist."

Truman Capote

"I'm what you call a teleological existential atheist. I believe that there's an intelligence to the universe with the exception of certain parts of New Jersey."

Woody Allen

"I wonder if anybody ever reached the age of 35 in New England without wanting to kill himself."

Writer Barrett Wendell

"If God had meant for Texans to ski, he would have made bullshit white."

Anonymous

"If I owned Texas and Hell, I would rent out Texas and live in Hell."

General Philip H. Sheridan

"The only thing that smells worse than an oil refinery is a feedlot. Texas has a lot of both."

Molly Ivins

AMERICAN CITIES

. . . .

"There are two million interesting people in New York—
and only seventy-eight in Los Angeles."

Neil Simon

"[Los Angeles is] seventy-two suburbs in search of a city."

Dorothy Parker

"The difference between Los Angeles and yogurt is that yogurt has real culture."

Tom Taussik

"What does it feel like to be dead for 200 years? Like spending a weekend in Beverly Hills."

Woody Allen, in Sleeper

"Hollywood—an emotional Detroit."

Lillian Gish

"Hollywood is like being nowhere and talking to nobody about nothing."

Michelangelo Antonioni

"Hollywood is the only place where you can wake up in the morning and hear the birds coughing in the trees."

Vaudevillian Joe Frisco

"In Hollywood, if you don't have happiness, you send out for it."

Rex Reed

"I've been asked if I ever get the DTs. I don't know; it's hard to tell where Hollywood ends and the DTs begin."

W. C. Fields

Hollywood:
"The only place in the world where a man can get stabbed in the back while climbing a ladder."

William Faulkner

Roseanne on Hollywood:
"This town is a back-stabbing, scum-sucking, small-minded town, but thanks for the money."

"Hollywood is where the stars twinkle, then wrinkle."

Victor Mature

"What I like about Hollywood is that one can get along by knowing two words of English—swell and lousy."

Vicki Baum

"Hollywood is a place where your best friend will plunge a knife in your back and then call the police to tell them that you are carrying a concealed weapon."

George Frazier

"Strip the phony tinsel off Hollywood and you'll find the real tinsel underneath."

Oscar Levant

When Shirley Knight skipped the Oscar ceremony the year she was nominated for best supporting actress for *Sweet Bird of Youth,* she sneered, "Hollywood—that's where they give Academy Awards to Charlton Heston for acting."

"In Hollywood, all marriages are happy. It's trying to live together afterwards that causes the problems."

Shelley Winters

"God felt sorry for actors, so he created Hollywood to give them a place in the sun and a swimming pool. The price they had to pay was to surrender their talent."

Cedric Hardwicke

"A leader of public thought in Hollywood wouldn't have sufficient mental acumen anywhere else to hold down a place in a breadline."

Anita Loos

"Hollywood is a place where people from Iowa mistake each other for a star."

Fred Allen

"If you stay in Beverly Hills too long, you become a Mercedes."

Robert Redford

"Popcorn is the last area of the movie business where good taste is still a concern."

Journalist Mike Barfield

"You can take all the sincerity in Hollywood, place it in the navel of a fruit fly, and still have room enough for three caraway seeds and a producer's heart."

Fred Allen

"The only 'ism' Hollywood really believes in is plagiarism."

Dorothy Parker

"Nothing important has ever come out of San Francisco. Rice-A-Roni aside."

Michael O'Donoghue

"A car is useless in New York, essential everywhere else. The same with good manners."

Mignon McLaughlin

"New York: the only city where people make radio requests like 'This is for Tina—I'm sorry I stabbed you.' "

Carol Leifer

"[New York:] The city of right angles and tough, damaged people."

Pete Hamill

"[New York City] is the most exciting place in the world to live. There are so many ways to die here."

Denis Leary

"New York is the only city in the world where you can get deliberately run down on the sidewalk by a pedestrian."

Russell Baker

"The trouble with New York is that it has no nationality at all. It is simply a sort of free port—a place where the raw materials of civilization are received, sorted out, and sent further on."

H. L. Mencken

"Miami Beach is where neon goes to die."
Lenny Bruce

"[Philadelphia has] all the filth and corruption of a big city [and] all the pettiness and insularity of a small town."
Howard Ogden

"When an Omaha man (or boy) speaks of a steak, one expects him to pull from his pocket a series of treasured snapshots of steaks."
Writer Philip Hamburger

"Detroit is Cleveland without the glitter."
Anonymous

Hunter S. Thompson on Chicago:
"This vicious, stinking zoo, this mean-grinning, Mace-smelling boneyard of a city: an elegant rockpile of a monument to everything cruel and stupid and corrupt in the human spirit."

"[Washington, D.C.] is too small to be a state but too large to be an asylum for the mentally deranged."
*Former EPA administrator
Anne Burford*

"Washington is a city of Southern efficiency and Northern charm."
John F. Kennedy

A social snob once asked James Whistler, "Whatever possessed you to be born in a place like Lowell, Massachusetts?" Whistler's reply: "I wished to be near my mother."

"I have just returned from Boston. It is the only thing to do if you find yourself up there."

Fred Allen

MANNERS

. . . .

When accosted by a man who insisted he knew him, Groucho Marx said, "I never forget a face, but in your case I'll make an exception."

"I have a previous engagement, which I will make as soon as possible."

John Barrymore

"Good breeding consists of concealing how much we think of ourselves and how little we think of the other person."

Mark Twain

"Let us make a special effort to stop communicating with each other, so we can have some conversation."

Miss Manners

"He's the kind of guy who can brighten a room by leaving it."

Milton Berle

"Santa Claus has the right idea: Visit people once a year."
Victor Borge

"Conversation is the enemy of good wine and food."
Alfred Hitchcock

"The nice thing about being a celebrity is that when you bore people, they think it's their fault."
Henry Kissinger

"I enjoyed talking to you. My mind needed a rest."
Henny Youngman

"His table manners are atrocious. I know chicken can be eaten with your fingers, but not when it's in soup."
Humorist Gene Perret

"Never strike anyone so old, small, or weak that verbal abuse would have sufficed."

P. J. O'Rourke, in Modern Manners

"A good listener is usually thinking about something else."
Elbert Hubbard

"It's gotten so that if a man opens a door for a lady to go through first, he's the doorman."
Mae West

"Winston, you are drunk," Bessie Braddock pointed out to Churchill, who replied, "Indeed, Madam, and you are ugly, but tomorrow I'll be sober."

POLITICS AND POLITICIANS

. . . .

"All politics are based on the indifference of the majority."
James Reston

"The first requirement of a statesman is that he be dull. This is not always easy to achieve."
Dean Acheson

"Take our politicians: They're a bunch of yo-yos. The presidency is now a cross between a popularity contest and a high school debate, with an encyclopedia of clichés the first prize."
Saul Bellow

"If hypocrisy were gold, the Capitol would be Fort Knox."
Senator John McCain

"A politician is a man who understands government and it takes a politician to run a government. A statesman is a politician who's been dead ten or fifteen years."
Harry S. Truman

"A politician is a person with whose politics you don't agree; if you agree with him he is a statesman."
David Lloyd George

"You can't use tact with a congressman. A congressman is a hog. You must take a stick and hit him on the snout."
Henry Adams

"[Congressmen] never open their mouths without subtracting from the sum of human knowledge."
Speaker of the House Thomas Reed

"[William McKinley] had about as much backbone as a chocolate eclair."
Theodore Roosevelt

"Just say the word 'politician' and I think of chicanery."
Lucille Ball

"Have you ever seen a candidate talking to a rich person on television?"
Art Buchwald

"He has all the characteristics of a dog except loyalty."
American politician Sam Houston
on Thomas Jefferson Green

"Fleas can be taught nearly anything that a congressman can."
Mark Twain

Margot Asquith on the Earl of Birkenhead:
"He is very clever, but sometimes he lets his brains go to his head."

A woman once accosted Churchill with:
"There are two things I don't like about you, Mr. Churchill—your politics and your moustache." Without hesitation, Churchill replied, "My dear madam, pray do not disturb yourself. You are not likely to come into contact with either."

British politician Aneurin Bevan on Churchill:
"His ear is so sensitively attuned to the bugle note of history that he is often deaf to the more raucous clamor of modern life."

George Bernard Shaw invited Churchill to the opening night of his new play, *St. Joan,* in 1923. Churchill replied, "I cannot come. Would it be possible for you to let me have tickets for the second night—if there is one?" Shaw retorted, "Bring a friend, if you have one."

"If you weren't such a great man, you'd be a terrible bore."
Mrs. William Gladstone, to her husband,
the British prime minister

British politician Nicholas Fairbairn on Prime Minister Edward Heath:
"A little boy sucking his misogynistic thumb and blubbing and carping in the corner of the front bench below the gangway is a mascot which Parliament can do without."

"[Heath is] a shiver looking for a spine to run up."
Prime Minister Harold Wilson

"They told me how Mr. Gladstone read Homer for fun, which I thought served him right."
Winston Churchill

"If Gladstone fell into the Thames, that would be a misfortune, and if anybody pulled him out, that, I suppose, would be a calamity."
Earl of Beaconsfield Benjamin Disraeli,
when asked to distinguish between a
misfortune and a calamity

"[Gladstone] has not a single redeeming defect."
Benjamin Disraeli

Australian prime minister Paul Keating referred to an attack by Opposition leader John Hewson:
"Like being flogged with a warm lettuce."

"Some fellows get credit for being conservative when they are only stupid."

Elbert Hubbard

"A conservative is a man who is too cowardly to fight and too fat to run."

Elbert Hubbard

"Conservatives are not necessarily stupid, but most stupid people are conservatives."

John Stuart Mill

"A conservative is a liberal who got mugged the night before."

Frank Rizzo

"A conservative is someone who believes in reform. But not now."

Mort Sahl

"If God had been a liberal, we wouldn't have had the Ten Commandments—we'd have the Ten Suggestions."

Malcolm Bradbury

"You can fool too many of the people too much of the time."

James Thurber

"Governments last as long as the undertaxed can defend themselves against the overtaxed."

British art critic Bernard Berenson

"It is the function of government to invent philosophies to explain the demands of its own convenience."

American political analyst
Murray Kempton

"Politicians are the same all over. They promise to build a bridge even when there's no river."

Nikita Khrushchev

"A government that is big enough to give you all you want is big enough to take it all away."

Barry Goldwater

"Too bad all the people who know how to run the country are busy driving cabs and cutting hair."

George Burns

"Public office is the last refuge of the incompetent."

Boies Penrose

"The office of president is such a bastardized thing, half-royalty and half-democracy, that nobody knows whether to genuflect or spit."

Jimmy Breslin

"My choice early in life was either to be a piano player in a whorehouse or a politician. And to tell the truth, there's hardly any difference."

Harry S. Truman

"Being president is like being a jackass in a hailstorm: There's nothing to do but stand there and take it."

Lyndon B. Johnson

When Geoffrey Howe criticized him before the House of Commons, Denis Healy retorted that it was "like being savaged by a dead sheep."

"Congress is so strange. A man gets up to speak and says nothing. Nobody listens—and then everybody disagrees."

Boris Marshalov

"Suppose you were an idiot, and suppose you were a member of Congress. But I repeat myself."

Mark Twain

"John Major, Norman Lamont: I wouldn't spit in their mouths if their teeth were on fire."

Rodney Bickerstaffe, UNISON

"I decided the worst thing you can call Paul Keating, quite frankly, is Paul Keating."

*Australian politician John Hewson,
on the Australian Labour
prime minister*

British politician Herbert Samuel on the civil service: "A difficulty for every solution."

"He knows nothing and thinks he knows everything. That points clearly to a political career."

George Bernard Shaw

"Far better to keep your mouth shut and let everyone think you're stupid than to open it and leave no doubt."

British politician Norman Tebbit

Margot Asquith on Prime Minister David Lloyd George: "He could not see a belt without hitting below it."

"When they circumcised Herbert Samuel, they threw away the wrong bit."

Prime Minister David Lloyd George
on a fellow politician

"[Warren Harding's] speeches leave the impression of an army of pompous phrases moving over the landscape in search of an idea. Sometimes these meandering words would actually capture a struggling thought and bear it triumphantly a prisoner in their midst until it died of servitude and overwork."

Senator William McAdoo

"[Theodore Roosevelt was] an old maid with testosterone poisoning."

American writer Patricia O'Toole

"Harding was not a bad man. He was just a slob."

Alice Roosevelt Longworth

"Calvin Coolidge didn't say much, and when he did he didn't say much."

Will Rogers

"[Franklin Roosevelt was] two-thirds mush and one-third Eleanor."

Alice Roosevelt Longworth

"[Franklin Roosevelt was] a chameleon on plaid."
Herbert Hoover

"The trouble with this country is that there are too many politicians who believe, with a conviction based on experience, that you can fool all of the people all of the time."
American journalist
Franklin P. Adams in 1944

"The truckman, the trashman, and the policeman on the corner may call me Alice, but you may not."
Alice Roosevelt Longworth,
to Senator Joseph McCarthy

Secretary of the Interior Harold Ickes on Harry S. Truman: "I am against government by crony."

"Harry Truman proves that old adage that any man can become president of the United States."
American socialist Norman Thomas

"Adlai Stevenson was a man who could never make up his mind whether he had to go to the bathroom or not."
Harry S. Truman

"As an intellectual, [Dwight Eisenhower] bestowed upon the games of golf and bridge all the enthusiasm and perseverance that he withheld from his books and ideas."

Emmet John Hughes

John F. Kennedy on Everett Dirksen:
"The Wizard of Ooze."

William F. Buckley Jr. on Lyndon Johnson:
"He is a man of his most recent word."

"Bobby Kennedy and Nelson Rockefeller are having a row, ostensibly over the plight of New York's mentally retarded, a loose definition of which would include everyone in New York who voted for Kennedy or Rockefeller."

William F. Buckley Jr.

Murray Kempton on Robert Kennedy:
"The highest ranking withdrawn adolescent since Alexander Hamilton in 1794."

"Nixon is the kind of politician who would cut down a red-wood tree and then mount the stump to make a speech for conservation."

Adlai Stevenson

"The Eichmann trial taught the world the banality of evil; now Nixon is teaching the world the evil of banality."

I. F. Stone

"[Nixon] told us he was going to take crime out of the streets. He did. He took it into the damn White House."

Ralph Abernathy

"For years I've regarded [Nixon's] very existence as a monument to all the rancid genes and broken chromosomes that corrupt the possibilities of the American Dream; he was a foul caricature of himself, a man with no soul, no inner convictions, with the integrity of a hyena and the style of a poison toad."

Hunter S. Thompson

"Nixon is a shifty-eyed, goddamn, lying son-of-a-bitch, and people know it. He's one of the few in the history of the country to run for high office talking out of both sides of his mouth at the same time—and lying out of both sides."

Harry S. Truman

"It was hard to listen to Goldwater and realize that a man could be half-Jewish and yet sometimes appear twice as dense as the normal gentile."

I. F. Stone

"[Gerald Ford] looks and talks as if he just fell off Edgar Bergen's lap."

David Steinberg

"Jimmy Carter as president is like Truman Capote marrying Dolly Parton. The job is too big for him."

Rich Little

"Jimmy Hoffa's most valuable contribution to the American labor movement came at the moment he stopped breathing on July 3, 1975."

Journalist Dan E. Moldea

"I can still remember the first time I ever heard Hubert Humphrey speak. He was in the second hour of a five-minute talk."

Gerald Ford

Hunter S. Thompson called Hubert Humphrey "a treacherous, gutless old ward-heeler who should be put in a bottle and sent out with the Japanese current."

"If you want to find a politician free of any influence, you can find Adolf Hitler, who made up his own mind."

Eugene McCarthy

Nixon had this to say about the Democratic presidential candidates of 1988:
"I've often said that the best politics is poetry rather than prose. [Jesse] Jackson is a poet. [Mario] Cuomo is a poet. And Dukakis is a word processor."

"*Dukakis* is Greek for *Mondale.*"
Jay Leno

"Congress—these, for the most part, illiterate hacks whose fancy vests are spotted with gravy and whose speeches, hypocritical, unctuous, and slovenly, are spotted also with the gravy of political patronage."
Mary McCarthy

"[Senator Ed] Muskie talked like a farmer with terminal cancer trying to borrow on next year's crop."
Hunter S. Thompson

"The liberals like [John F. Kennedy's] rhetoric and the conservatives like his inaction."
American socialist Norman Thomas

"I admire Ted Kennedy. How many 59-year-olds do you know who still go to Florida for spring break?"
Patrick Buchanan

"Senator McGovern was making a speech. He said, 'Gentlemen, let me tax your memories.' And Ted Kennedy jumped up and said, 'Why haven't we thought of that before?'"

Bob Dole

"I don't understand guys who call themselves feminists. That's like the time Hubert Humphrey, running for president, told a black audience he was a soul brother."

Roy Blount Jr.

"Bobby Kennedy is so concerned about poverty because he didn't have any as a kid."

Ronald Reagan

"[Ronald Reagan is] a triumph of the embalmer's art."

Gore Vidal

"[Ronald Reagan is] so shockingly dumb that by his very presence in the office he numbs an entire country."

Jimmy Breslin

"That youthful sparkle in [Reagan's] eye is caused by his contact lenses, which he keeps highly polished."

Sheila Graham

"I'm glad that Reagan is President. Of course, I'm a professional comedian."

Will Durst

"George Bush is Gerald Ford without the pizzazz."
Pat Paulsen

"I listen to Reagan and I want to throw up."
Henry Fonda

"I believe that Ronald Reagan can make this country what it once was—an Arctic region covered with ice."
Steve Martin

When Mary Travers, of the trio Peter, Paul and Mary, was invited by the Reagan White House to the annual Easter egg roll, she retorted, "I don't want to roll an egg with Ronald Reagan. I want to throw one at him."

"Washington could not tell a lie; Nixon could not tell the truth; Reagan cannot tell the difference."
Mort Sahl

"Just as with yoga, in order to truly excel at not blinking, you must begin by letting your mind be perfectly empty. The right sport for Ronald Reagan."
Molly Ivins, after Senator Richard Lugar said that Reagan "didn't blink" during arms control talks with Gorbachev

"We've got the kind of President [in Reagan] who thinks arms control means some kind of deodorant."

Patricia Schroeder

"William Bennett, who had been secretary of education without solving the problems of education and drug czar without solving the problems of drugs, now wants to write a book on how to solve the problems of both. In America, this is what we call 'expertise.' "

Baltimore Sun *columnist Roger Simon*

Commentator Jim Hightower on George Bush:
"A toothache of a man."

"[George Bush is] a Boy Scout with a hormone imbalance."

Republican analyst Kevin Phillips

"George Bush was born with a silver foot in his mouth."

Governor Ann Richards

"[Dan Quayle] thinks that *Roe v. Wade* are two ways to cross the Potomac."

Patricia Schroeder

"Dan Quayle is so dumb he thinks Cheerios are doughnut seeds."

Jim Hightower

Professor William Cavanaugh said, of his former student Dan Quayle, "I looked into those blue eyes, and I might have been looking out the window."

"[Dan Quayle] seems like the average type of man. He's not, like, smart. I'm not trying to rag on him or anything. But he has the same mentality I have—and I'm in the eighth grade."

Student Vanessa Martinez

"If a tree fell in a forest and no one was there to hear it, it might sound like Dan Quayle looks."

Tom Shales

"Nobody likes to be called a liar. But to be called a liar by Bill Clinton is really a unique experience."

Ross Perot

After media consultant Roger Ailes called Ross Perot "a nutcase," Perot suggested that the corpulent Ailes "needs to go on Slim Fast." Ailes retorted, "I could drink some Slim Fast, lose a few pounds. But when they lower his scrawny little rear end into the ground, he's still going to be nuts."

After Perot addressed the NAACP as "you people," Arsenio Hall said, on his talk show, "Personally, Mr. Perot, if you're watching, I wasn't offended, you no-platform-having, inch-high private eye, *Dukes of Hazzard*–sounding, gay-bashing, flip-flopping, got-a-million-dollars-in-the-bank-and-still-go-to-Super-Cuts-to-show-off-them-big-Dumbo-ears-of-corn, I wasn't offended at all."

"Bill Clinton's foreign policy experience stems mainly from having breakfast at the International House of Pancakes."
Pat Buchanan

"Al Gore is in danger of becoming all things to no people."
Paul Bogard, Michael Dukakis's campaign manager

Slick Times founder Michael Dalton Johnson told the *Los Angeles Times* that having to choose among Bush, Clinton, and Perot was like needing a pair of underpants but being forced to "decide between three dirty pairs."

"Being attacked on ethics by Al D'Amato is like being called ugly by a frog."
DNC chairman David Wilhelm, on D'Amato's attack on Clinton during the Whitewater affair

"What do you do if you're in a room with Muammar Qaddafi, Saddam Hussein, and John Sununu, and you have a gun that has only two bullets? Shoot Sununu twice."

Michael Dukakis

"Being in politics is like being a football coach: You have to be smart enough to understand the game, and dumb enough to think it's important."

Eugene McCarthy

Harold Macmillan on Prime Minister Anthony Eden:
"He is forever poised between a cliché and an indiscretion."

British politician Reginald Paget on Eden:
"An overripe banana, yellow outside, squishy in."

British politician Jonathan Aitken on Margaret Thatcher:
"She probably thinks Sinai is the plural of sinus."

British writer Clement Freud on Thatcher:
"Attila the Hen."

Australian critic Clive James on Thatcher:
"She sounded like the book of Revelation read out over a railway public address system by a headmistress of a certain age wearing calico knickers."

Barry Goldwater on politician William Scott:
"If he were any dumber, he'd be a tree."

"I think the last book Nancy Reagan read was *Black Beauty*."

Roger Straus

Barbara Ehrenreich called Nancy Reagan "a senescent bimbo with a lust for home furnishings."

Frank Sinatra on Nancy Reagan:
"A dope with fat ankles."

"I think that Nancy [Reagan] does most of [Ronald Reagan's] talking; you'll notice that she never drinks water when Ronnie speaks."

Robin Williams

"[Nancy Reagan] has shrunk lately, just like George Burns. Nancy's gotten older before our eyes, and she's shrunk out of meanness. Oh, she's a mean woman."

Mr. Blackwell, compiler of the "worst-dressed" lists

"The idea of Prince Charles conversing with vegetables is not quite so amusing when you remember that he's had plenty of practice chatting to members of his own family."

Journalist Jaci Stephens,
The Sunday Times (*London*)

After Congressman Dan Burton, chairman of the Committee on Government Reform, referred to President Bill Clinton as a "scumbag," White House Spokesman Mike McCurry retorted, "The use of a two-syllable vulgarity by the chairman was rather ambitious."

SPORTS

"Golf is a good walk spoiled."
Mark Twain

"I regard golf as an expensive way of playing marbles."
G. K. Chesterton

"They thought lacrosse was what you found in la church."
Robin Williams

"He couldn't hit a curveball with an ironing board."
*Pitcher Bob Feller on Michael Jordan's bid
to play for the Chicago White Sox*

"Defensively the Red Sox are a lot like Stonehenge. They are old, they don't move, and no one is certain why they are positioned the way they are."
Sportswriter Dan Shaughnessy

"He has never taken a shot that he couldn't miss."
Sportswriter Paul Ladewski on
Cleveland Cavaliers guard Gerald Wilkins

"I believe every human has a finite number of heartbeats. I don't intend to waste any of mine running around doing exercises."
Neil Armstrong

"The need of exercise is a modern superstition, invented by people who ate too much and had nothing to think about. Athletics don't make anybody either long-lived or useful."
George Santayana

"If I ever needed a brain transplant, I'd choose a sportswriter because I'd want a brain that had never been used."
Norm Van Brocklin

Florida State football coach Bobby Bowden on linebacker Reggie Herring:
"He doesn't know the meaning of the word 'fear.' In fact, I just saw his grades and he doesn't know the meaning of a lot of words."

"They had better defense at Pearl Harbor."
Pittsburgh Pirates center fielder Andy Van
Slyke on his team

"Baseball is supposed to be a noncontact sport, but our hitters seem to be taking that literally."

Pirates manager Larry Doughty

"It's said that swimming develops poise and grace, but have you seen how a duck walks?"

Woody Allen

"I squirm when I see athletes praying before a game. Don't they realize that if God took sports seriously He would never have created George Steinbrenner?"

Mark Russell

"Golf is a lot of walking, broken up by disappointment and bad arithmetic."

Mark Twain

"The English country gentleman galloping after a fox: the unspeakable in full pursuit of the uneatable."

Oscar Wilde

"Joggers are basically neurotic, bony, smug types who could bore the paint off a DC-10. It is a scientifically proven fact that having to sit through a three-minute conversation between two joggers will cause your IQ to drop 13 points."

Rick Reilly,
in Sports Illustrated

"Runners, people who actually run in marathons, just look pathetic to me. It can't be worth it. They look like those people in the health-food store: gray pallor, stringy little beards, sunken chests. They make you want to call 911."

Calvin Trillin

"It's unnatural for people to run around city streets unless they are thieves or victims. It makes people nervous to see someone running. I know that when I see someone running on my street, my instincts tell me to let the dog out after them."

Mike Royko

"He likes to complain about not playing [baseball], which is what he does best—not play."

*Player Pat Gillick
on pitcher Mike
Marshall*

"We don't need [basketball] refs, but I guess white guys need something to do."

Charles Barkley

"Seeing Yankees fans up close for the first time is like waking up in a Brazilian jail."

Umpire Art Hill

"The word 'aerobics' comes from two Greek words: *aero*, meaning 'ability to,' and *bics*, meaning 'withstand tremendous boredom.' "

Dave Barry

"When Muhammad Ali was born, he was a six-pound mouth."

Bob Hope

RELIGION

. . . .

"No man with any sense of humor ever founded a religion."
Robert G. Ingersoll

"Religion is the fashionable substitute for belief."
Oscar Wilde

"Randomness scares people. Religion is a way to explain randomness."
Fran Lebowitz

"Going to church doesn't make you a Christian any more than going to the garage makes you a car."
Laurence J. Peter

"Perhaps the most lasting pleasure in life is the pleasure of not going to church."
William Inge

"If you talk to God, you are praying; if God talks to you, you have schizophrenia."

Thomas Szasz

"Christ died for our sins. Dare we make his martyrdom meaningless by not committing them?"

Jules Feiffer

"The Bible tells us to love our neighbors, and also to love our enemies; probably because they are generally the same people."

G. K. Chesterton

"Organized Christianity has probably done more to retard the ideals that were its founders' than any other agency in the world."

Richard Le Gallienne

"Don't stay away from church because there are so many hypocrites. There's always room for one more."

A. R. Adams

"I went to a convent in New York and was fired finally for my insistence that the Immaculate Conception was spontaneous combustion."

Dorothy Parker

"Puritanism [is] the haunting fear that someone, somewhere, may be happy."

H. L. Mencken

"All religions are founded on the fear of the many and the cleverness of the few."

Stendhal

"Confession is good for the soul only in the sense that a tweed coat is good for dandruff—it is a palliative rather than a remedy."

Peter De Vries

"Not only is there no God, but try getting a plumber on weekends."

Woody Allen

"Religion is a monumental chapter in the history of human egotism."

William James

"The trouble with born-again Christians is that they are an even bigger pain the second time around."

Herb Caen

"[Reverend Billy] Graham has, with great self-discipline, turned himself into the thinking man's Easter bunny."

Garry Wills

"Please, O ye Lord, keep Jim Bakker behind bars."

Dana Carvey

As she put money into a Salvation Army worker's outstretched tambourine, Tallulah Bankhead said, "Don't bother to thank me. I know what a perfectly ghastly season it's been for you Spanish dancers."

"A convent is a place of retirement for women who wish for leisure to meditate upon the vice of idleness."

Ambrose Bierce

"A casual stroll through the lunatic asylum shows that faith does not prove anything."

Friedrich Nietzsche

"It is usually when men are at their most religious that they behave with the least sense and the greatest cruelty."

Ilka Chase

"When a man is freed of religion, he has a better chance to live a normal and wholesome life."

Sigmund Freud

"After coming in contact with a religious man, I always feel that I must wash my hands."

Friedrich Nietzsche

"A dead atheist is someone who's all dressed up with no place to go."

James Duffecy

"There are three sexes—men, women, and clergymen."
Sydney Smith

"God is love, but get it in writing."

Gypsy Rose Lee

"The only excuse for God is that he doesn't exist."
Stendhal

"The chief contribution of Protestantism to human thought is its massive proof that God is a bore."

H. L. Mencken

"A Puritan is a person who pours righteous indignation into the wrong things."

G. K. Chesterton

"The idea of a Supreme Being who creates a world in which one creature is designed to eat another in order to subsist, and then passes a law saying, 'Thou shalt not kill,' is so monstrously, immeasurably, bottomlessly absurd that I am at a loss to understand how mankind has entertained or given it house room all this long."

Peter De Vries

"The last Christian died on the cross."

Friedrich Nietzsche

"If Jesus were to come today, people would not even crucify him. They would ask him to dinner, and hear what he had to say, and make fun of him."

Thomas Carlyle

"Every day people are straying away from the church and going back to God."

Lenny Bruce

"Sudden conversion is particularly attractive to the half-baked mind."

E. M. Forster

"Many people think they have religion when they are troubled with dyspepsia."

Robert G. Ingersoll

"Religion is excellent stuff for keeping common people quiet."

Napoleon Bonaparte